ARCHAEOLOGICAL SURVEY OF WESTERN INDIA

REPORT

OF THE

FIRST SEASON'S OPERATIONS

IN THE

BELGAM AND KALADGI DISTRICTS.

JANUARY TO MAY 1874.

ARCHAEOLOGICAL SURVEY OF WESTERN INDIA

REPORT
OF THE
FIRST SEASON'S OPERATIONS
IN THE
BELGAM AND KALADGI DISTRICTS.

JANUARY TO MAY 1874.

BY

JAMES BURGESS, ESQ., M.R.A.S., F.R.G.S.,
MEMBRE DE LA SOCIETE ASIATIQUE,
ARCHAEOLOGICAL SURVEYOR AND REPORTER TO GOVERNMENT,

EDITOR OF "THE INDIAN ANTIQUARY;" AUTHOR OF "THE ROCK-TEMPLES OF ELEPHANTA." "ARCHITECTURE AND SCENERY IN GUJARAT AND RAJPUTANA," ETC.

GYAN

Published by

Gyan Publishing House
5, Ansari Road
Daryaganj, New Delhi-110002
Phone: 011-47034999, 9811692060
E-mail: books@gyanbooks.com

Distribution Network
gyanbooks.com
India, USA, Canada, UK, Australia, France

ISBN : 978-81-212-2117-7 (HB)
First Published, 1874

2nd Impression 2021

Printed at: Gyan Press, Delhi.

Report of the First Season's Operations
in the
Belgam and Kaladgi Districts.
Author: James Burgess

ARCHÆOLOGICAL SURVEY OF WESTERN INDIA.

REPORT

OF THE

FIRST SEASON'S OPERATIONS

IN THE

BELGÂM AND KALADGI DISTRICTS.

JANUARY TO MAY 1874.

BY

JAMES BURGESS, Esq., M.R.A.S., F.R.G.S.,

MEMBRE DE LA SOCIÉTÉ ASIATIQUE,

ARCHÆOLOGICAL SURVEYOR AND REPORTER TO GOVERNMENT,

EDITOR OF "THE INDIAN ANTIQUARY;" AUTHOR OF "THE ROCK-TEMPLES OF ELEPHANTA," "ARCHITECTURE AND SCENERY IN GUJARAT AND RAJPUTANA," ETC.

LONDON:

INDIA MUSEUM,

1874.

Wm. H. ALLEN AND CO., 13, WATERLOO PLACE, S.W.

Publishers to the India Office.

CONTENTS.

ILLUSTRATIONS.

PREFATORY LETTER.

TO THE CHIEF SECRETARY TO GOVERNMENT, BOMBAY.

SIR, 22, *Seton Place, Edinburgh*, July 1874.

I HAVE the honour to submit the accompanying Report on the Archæological Survey of the Bombay Presidency for the past season.

This Survey originated in the Despatch of the Bombay Government No. $\frac{2592}{108 G.}$ of 24th July 1873 accompanying the Minute of the Honourable J. Gibbs, C.S., of 25th June, suggesting arrangements for carrying into effect the proposals made in the Despatch of His Grace the Secretary of State for India—No. 173, of 11th Oct. 1871.

2. The scheme proposed by the Honourable Mr. Gibbs and approved by the Government of Bombay contemplated my employment to survey the whole of the Cave Temples of Western India, including also surveys of some at least of the more interesting Brahmanical and Jaina remains. The field indicated in this Minute, including, as it did, Ajaṇṭâ, Elora, and other groups of caves, &c. in the Haidarâbâd territory, fully met the main object of the Despatch of 11th October 1871, and allowed of my utilizing the whole of the collections I had made privately in preceding years. The Government of India, however, in sanctioning the scheme of the Honourable Mr. Gibbs, introduced a clause limiting the area of research to the Bombay Presidency only, thus cutting off Ajaṇṭâ and other groups of caves just outside the limits of the Presidency, and so rendering impossible the contemplated production of a complete work on the "Rock-Cut Temples of Western India." This limitation, however, I have no doubt will be reconsidered.

3. The sanction of the Government of India was finally given on 9th September last, and, on consultation with Mr. J. Fergusson, I decided to devote the first season,—being a very short one,—to the Kanarese districts, surveying the Caves at Badâmi and Aiwaḷḷi (or *Iwullee*), of which hitherto so very little was satisfactorily known, together with the ancient Jaina and Brahmanical Temples at Belgâm, Paṭṭadkal (or *Purudkal*), and Aiwaḷḷi, visiting also such other of the places mentioned in the lists A 12 and B 12,

attached to my "Memorandum" of 24th Aug. 1870,* as might be easily accessible. From this district, a number of the photographs, in the third volume—that on Dharwar and Mysore,—published by the Committee of Architectural Antiquities of Western India, in 1866, had been obtained; but, unlike the volume on Bijapoor, these photographs were unaccompanied by any plans or descriptive notes taken on the spot to make them intelligible. Of the ninety-eight photographs in that volume, Nos. XLV., LII.-LXI., LXX.-LXXIII., LXXXVIII., and XCIV. are from places noticed in the following Report, and complement the series I have taken.

4. I returned to Bombay and took charge of the duties of the office of Archæological Surveyor and Reporter on the 15th January last.

5. With the very limited means at my disposal the organization of anything like a proper staff and within the space of a few days was almost impossible. I lost no time, however, in calling on Mr. Terry, the Superintendent of the Bombay School of Art, and in making private inquiry for assistants. One of the best students of the School of Art was sick, but another was offered. He proved willing enough but exceedingly slow at his work, and came far short of my expectations as to style and finish. The allowance set down for photography (Rs. 1,500 for the year, or Rs. 250 a month for six months) was manifestly inadequate; it would do little more than pay for materials, &c., but I hoped that by using for this purpose a portion of the other allowances for establishment, and by doing everything I possibly could with my own hands, I might make it suffice. I could hear of no one likely to accept the terms I could offer for the photography, and I therefore employed an assistant moderately acquainted with the processes, and took charge of it myself. This is consequently the department in which the work has suffered most from insufficient funds, though the lenses, camera, &c. were provided free of expense to Government. The Honourable Mr. Gibbs, in paragraph 24 of his Minute, and the Government of Bombay, in paragraph 2 of the Despatch accompanying it, had suggested somewhat more liberal allowances, but such were not granted.

6. This staff of two assistants and a servant to clean glass plates, &c. was insufficient for the purposes of the Survey: the staff ought to consist of at least,—

(*a.*) Two School of Art students with some training for the work, so as to make copies of a fair proportion of the sculpture and architectural detail most deserving of attention.

(*b.*) A competent photographer.

(*c.*) A Pandit acquainted with the inscriptions and able to make copies of them.

Such a staff might be employed at only a slight increase on the present allowances, and

* "Memorandum on the Survey of Architectural and other Archæological Remains, with Lists of the Rock "Excavations, Temples, Mosques, &c. &c. in the Bombay Presidency, Sindh, Berar, Central Provinces, and "Haidarâbâd,"—addressed to the Honourable H. Pendock St. G. Tucker, C.S., Member of Council, and printed by order of Government.

would enable me to do the same amount of work at any given place in *half* the time and in a better style.

7. For the very important branch of inscriptions it would be of the greatest service in future, if I had the aid of a qualified Pandit, like Mr. Bhagwanlal Indraji, who has of late been supported by the munificence of the Junâgarh Darbâr to collect inscriptions for the illustration of the ancient history of the country, and who might be most profitably employed under my direction. I mention this here because, if such a person had accompanied me on my late expedition, what I regard as one of its shortcomings would have been avoided.

8. For the inscriptions I fully counted on being able to obtain the use, at least, of the volume of photographed inscriptions from the Kanarese Districts, edited by T. C. Hope, Esq., C.S., and published by the Committee of Architectural Antiquities of Western India in 1866, which would have been of the greatest service to me in showing what had already been satisfactorily done, what had better be recopied, and, indirectly, what other inscriptions might be copied, perhaps, for the first time. No copy of this important work, however, was to be found in the Secretariat,—nor is there a copy in the Library of the India Office. The Bombay Asiatic Society's copy had been lent without the permission of the committee, and I failed to obtain a sight of it. This I now regret the more as I have discovered that, in one case at least, I have missed one of the most valuable inscriptions it contains, and which is imperfectly photographed in it: not having the book to show what like and where it was, I mistook another for it.

9. All the inscriptions copied had to be done by my own hand, and I was often obliged to pass numbers of them, that might be of the greatest interest, simply because I could not spare the time to copy them.

10. As indicated in the Report the time in the field was limited. The work was actually commenced at Belgâm on 2nd February and concluded at Aiwaḷḷi on 16th April, in which time also not less than 200 miles were travelled, mostly over very rough country roads, in country carts, with such fragile baggage as photographic chemicals and glass. Besides this we had 230 miles more between Vingorla and Belgâm and from Aiwaḷḷi to Solapur. Under these circumstances and in so limited a time, it was impossible to accomplish all I could have wished to have done, but I trust the amount of work narrated in the accompanying report will not be deemed unsatisfactory or disappointing.

11. I have refrained from drawing conclusions respecting the remains visited, partly because it would extend to undue limits the present report,—and I intend it to be regarded as only a provisional one, written hurriedly during the short period I have to spend in Europe; and partly, because I believe the materials in plans, sections, drawings, photographs, and inscriptions which I have collected, and to the preparation of which for publication my time has been almost exclusively devoted,—will enable

those who really interest themselves in their study to form pretty correct opinions for themselves as to the additions to our knowledge which they afford. They supply at least a new chapter in the history of Indian architecture from the sixth to the eighth or ninth century. But it must be borne in mind that these materials do not adequately represent the antiquities of the Kanarese country. They only open up a field that would amply repay a much wider and more detailed survey than I had the means or the time to make.

12. A list of fifty-four photographs taken, and sent home to the India House together with the "estampages" of inscriptions, is given at the conclusion of the Report. Of the photographs, twenty are inserted in the Report, with a selection from the drawings and most of the inscriptions.

I have the honour to be, Sir,

Your most obedient servant,

JAS. BURGESS,

Archæological Surveyor and Reporter.

On special duty.

PLATE I.

BELGÂM - JAINA TEMPLE IN THE FORT No. I.

REPORT

OF THE

OPERATIONS OF THE ARCHÆOLOGICAL SURVEY

OF THE

BOMBAY PRESIDENCY.

15TH JANUARY TO MAY 1874.

THE present Report is not intended to be a final account of the Antiquities visited; it is rather of the nature of a journal of the work done during a short tour to a number of places in the valleys of the Ghaṭprabhâ and Mâlaprabhâ rivers in the Belgâm and Kalâdgi Zillas. The first place visited was Belgâm; from thence I proceeded northwards, by Ankalgi and Gokâk to Konur, and after a short stay there, returned by Hukeri to Belgâm, then went southward to Kâdaroḷi on the Mâlaprabhâ, and thence to Sampgânw, Bail-Hangal Saundati, Yellamâ, Hulî, and Manauli. Passing from Manauli to the north east, I next visited and examined the Badâmî Caves in the Kalâdgi district and went from them to Paṭṭadkal (the *Purudkal* of some visitors), and lastly to Aiwaḷḷi—the *Iwullee* and *Eiwally* of the older maps—where are both Cave-Temples and structural ones of great age and interest. This is the ground gone over. The time occupied from Belgâm to Aiwaḷḷi was eleven weeks. And in the following pages I submit the notes written down at the different places visited, with a selection of the drawings and photographs, rather than a digested account of the various architectural remains mentioned. When the systematic survey of the Antiquities in Western India is further advanced, it will be possible to present such an account in a connected form, so as to be more instructive from the greater area embraced.

With the very limited staff of one School-of-Art Student, an assistant for the photography and a plate-cleaner (as mentioned in paragraphs 5 and 6 of the preceding letter), I left Bombay on the 24th January and landed at Vingorla on the 25th. On the afternoon of the 29th we reached Belgâm; Friday and Saturday were spent in preparing the photographic chemicals, and roughly examining the old temples, &c.; and on Monday, 2nd February the survey was fairly started.

BELGÂM.

Within the Fort of Belgâm are three old Jaina temples, built, as indicated by the style, about the year 1200 A.D., a date confirmed by an inscription now in the Museum of the Bombay B. R. Asiatic Society, and said to have been carried off from one of these temples, by Major Jervis—but from which, I have as yet been unable to discover any record. This want of any statement as to the original position of inscriptions that have been removed by amateur archæologists is, in many cases, much to be regretted;

it sometimes deprives them of more than half their value, and ought to be very carefully guarded against. The inscription is of considerable length and is beautifully cut on a slab of black porphyry, unfortunately broken across. It is in the Hala Kânaḍâ language, and after the introductory sentence proceeds,—

"I adore Svasti and Śivabuddha Râja, the preserver and supporter of the Jaina "religion, who has brought under his rule the Devatas, the cow Kamdhenu, has "conquered the three passions; the soul of his disciples, whose breast is of vast "comprehension. In Jambudvîpa and Bharatkhaṇḍa, great among all kings, who "conquering all princes, established his throne firmly, such was Sena Râjâ; his son "was Kârtavîrya the great, powerful, the possessor of all virtues, the renowned; his "spouse was the beautiful Padmalladevî, ornamented with virtues; her son was called "Lakshmî-Bhupati; he was to his father and mother as Jayanta to Sachî and Purindra, "or as Shânmukha to Pârvatî and Śankara, as Manmâtha to Lakshmî and Nârâyaṇa,— "superior even to these, of higher merit. His wife Chandala Devî, had two sons, "Kali-Kârtavîrya and Malikârjuna, of valour and liberality, &c. . . . . Into "the mind of this Râjâ it entered to perform what would render him renowned among "those of this world, and in full enjoyment of his kingdom, residing at Venigrâma "(*Belgâm*) in peace and happiness,—he caused to be erected a temple, in which were "installed Śrî Santinâtha Deva* and the protectors of the eight points; for the "expenses of the annual festival-offerings, &c., of which temple, he gave, in Śaka 1127 "(A.D. 1205) Raktakshi Samvatsar, 2d Paush Śud, Wednesday, on the day of the "Makara Sankrânti, the village of Ambarvanni, &c."

This inscription, which is possibly one of the Ratta dynasty, should be published in facsimile, and a careful translation made of it.

One of the temples is inside the Commissariat compound, another is just outside, and the third—at a short distance—has been added to until it is no longer recognisable from outside, and is converted into quarters for married soldiers. There must have been other temples about the place, however; for many of the gateposts to houses both inside the Fort and outside are pillars from old Jaina temples. Two finely carved slabs were also dug up in a garden in camp last cold season: these ought, if possible, to be preserved in some place of safety. Indeed an empty bangalâ inside the Fort might surely be spared by Government in which to collect the nucleus of a small local museum. The district around is sufficiently rich in old sculptures and inscriptions to stock it within a very short time.

The shrine of the old temple outside the Commissariat (Plate I.) is entirely gone,—probably pulled down to allow the road to be carried straight past. The door of the shrine has been blocked up and the temple is used as a store by the Fort authorities. It consists of a porch the whole width of the building, with a screen wall in front, and of a *manḍap* —the hall or *naos*,† raised on sixteen pillars and as many pilasters. (See plan on Plate II.) The four central columns stand on a platform raised about $3\frac{1}{2}$ inches above the floor,—which platform the worshipper passes round to perform his devotions;—to approach

* The sixteenth of the twenty-four Jaina Tîrthañkaras or Jinas, sometimes called Arhaṇtas, and one of the five to whom temples are most frequently dedicated, the other four being Adiśvara or Rishabhanâtha, the first; and Neminâtha, Pârśvanâtha, and Mahâvira, the last three. Śântinâtha is distinguished by the cognizance (*chinha*) of an antelope (*mriga*) usually sculptured on his throne. (*See Indian Antiquary*, Vol. II. p. 138, and 140.)

† Conf. Râm Raj's *Essay*, p. 49.

BELGÂM-JAINA TEMPLE IN THE FORT No. I. PLATE II.

1

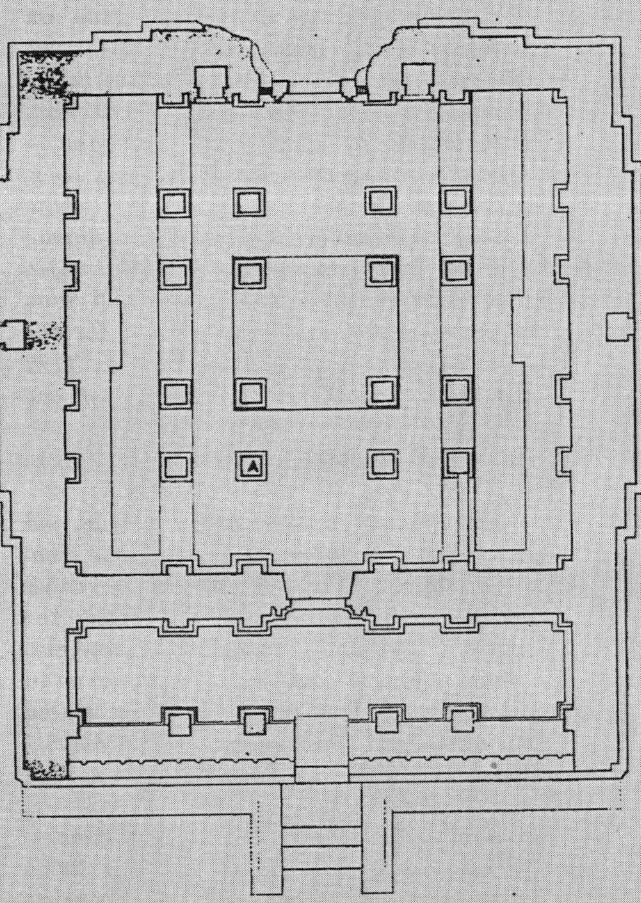

2

COLUMN. A. ON THE PLAN.

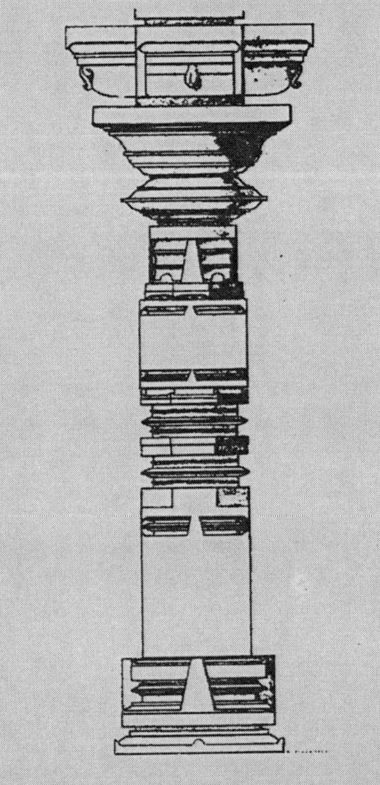

3

4

J. Burgess. delt.

W. Griggs, Photo-lith

BELGÂM-JAINA TEMPLE IN THE FORT No. II.

BELGÂM – JAINA TEMPLE IN THE FORT No. II. PLATE IV.

1. PLAN.

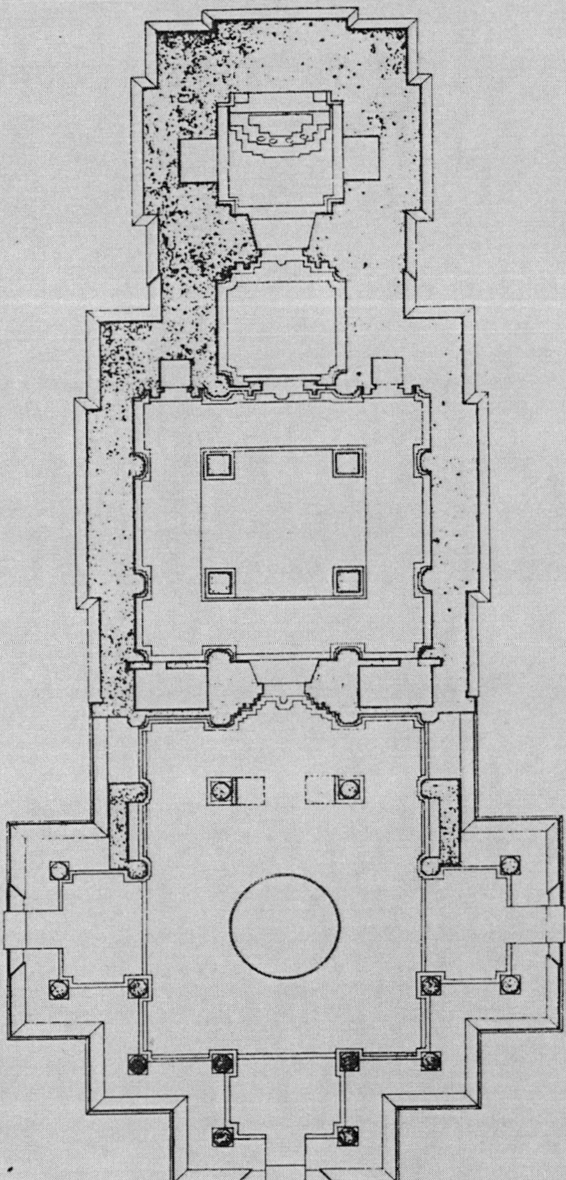

Burgess, delt.

Scale — Feet

2. COLUMN IN MANDAP.

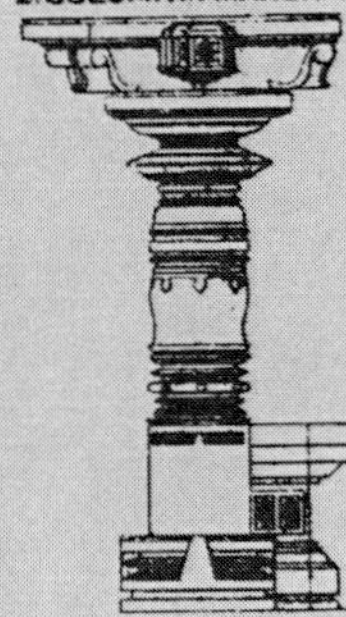

3.

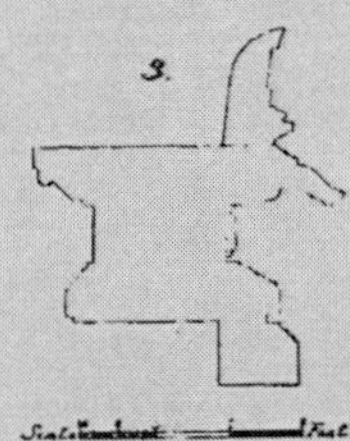

4.

straight forwards up to the presence of the god not being considered reverential. The side aisles have been separated from the central area by a latticed or perforated stone screen connecting the pillars; but of this only one piece—between the front wall and the first pillar of the right-hand row—now remains. There is a narrow plinth all along the side walls, and opposite the middle, it extends well forward as if for the seat of an image. Above this, about 5½ feet from the ground, is a stone shelf 18½ inches wide and 6 feet 4 inches long.

The stone beams over the columns are very massive, and those crossing the centre aisle have an opening over them nearly equal to their own depth, to allow the beams of the side aisles to overlap the bearings both in the central and outer aisle. Except the cobras on the capitals and four dancing satyrs on the door of the shrine now blocked up, there are no representations of living creature inside.

The door of the *maṇḍap* is of porphyry and delicately carved, but besmeared with paint, clay, &c. Over the centre is a kneeling figure and above the cornice are two others and two siñhas or lions. The verandah or porch is 14 feet 5 inches high in the middle and faces the south. The figures on the screen wall are almost all represented playing on musical instruments or dancing. The diamond-shaped ornaments below are very ingenious in device and all different: two examples of these are given in Plate II. figs. 3 and 4.

The shafts of the pillars are each a single stone, carved in the style represented in the drawing, Plate II. fig. 2; and some of the slabs in the walls measure 6 feet by 4, and in some instances even more. The foundations have sunk in some places producing cracks in the walls. The roof is overgrown by weeds and small trees, which must soon ruin it, if they are not speedily extirpated.

The large temple inside the Commissariat compound (see Plate III.) has also evidently been Jaina; but it is sometimes a matter of considerable difficulty to determine with certainty who were the builders of certain temples, for they have in many cases been appropriated by the Lingayat Śaivas and the original distinctive sculptures destroyed. This one consists of an open *maṇḍap* surmounted by a carefully carved dome, an inner temple or *shâla*, a small antechamber, and a shrine. It contains no image now, but in the shrine is the *asana* or throne for the idol, the back of which (quite black with smoke) is carved in representation of the usual cushion behind Jaina images; over this, on each side of the position for the head, a plant rises with many circular or wheel-shaped flowers. At the ends of the cushion are small colonettes supporting the back rail of the *asana* and a *siñha* or lion over a man (Plate IV. fig. 4); above this is an elephant with riders. At each side of the shrine is a deep niche in the wall.

The door is neatly carved, the outer line of sculpture being a series of small lions with grinning faces, each supporting his fellow above. Over the centre is a Jina with two fans, and on the very top are four *siñhas*. It is but little damaged.

The antechamber is plain with carved roof, the corners being cut off by four carved stones; the corners of the square thus formed are cut off by other four stones, and the central square filled by a stone carved with a lotus.

The door of this apartment is shewn in the photograph (Plate V.). On the under side of the cornice is carved a dancing figure between two musicians. Above is a damaged figure which, curiously enough, probably had eight arms. On each side of this door is a niche in the wall, neatly carved, and which probably were intended for figures of Jaina divinities or of the builders of the temple.

The pillars of the temple are square and massive but relieved by having all the principal facets, the triangles on the base and neck, carved with floral ornamentations. The roof of the central area between the four columns has been similar to that of the antechamber, but the central stone is gone. In the front wall of this chamber, which is 3 feet 7 inches thick, are two small recesses closed by sliding stones 1 foot 9 inches high.

The door leading from the Manḍap to the temple has been carved with uncommon care; unfortunately the engineer who repaired the temple a few years ago,—when, from the breaking of a lintel, it was in danger of falling in,—placed two very clumsy ashlar pillars, 2 feet square each, just in front of it, so that no satisfactory view of it can now be obtained. On the centre of the lintel is a *Tírthañkara* or sitting figure of a *Jina*, a deified Jaina teacher, and above the cornice are four squat human figures. On the neat colonettes of the jambs are five bands with human groups, in some of which the figures are little more than an inch high, yet in high relief; inside this is a band of rampant *siñhas* with a sort of high frill round the neck of each. Outside the colonettes is a band of *chakwas* or sacred geese, another of *siñhas*, and then one of human figures, mostly on bended knees.

The Manḍap is surrounded by a low screen wall, from which rise the pillars supporting the roof;—except the two in front of the door into the temple, the floor is thus almost free from pillars. Above the level of the screen, the pillars are round, with square bases, and are of a black sort of porphyry obtainable at no great distance, and which takes a high polish, and is strongly magnetic. A cobra's head forms the ornament on the ends of all the brackets. (See Plate IV. fig. 2.)

In each of the eight architraves which support the dome are carved five small *mandirs* or cells, each containing a squatting Jina, and between these are (four) *kausagiyas*—a sort of attendants or supporters, standing figures, each under a small canopy.

Over the brackets, which project inwards, there have been carved slabs: two on the north-east are gone; on one that remains, on the north, is a figure on horseback, with a high cap, a canopy or umbrella over his head, and a female behind him. The next is similar, but the animal's head is gone; the third animal is a *makara*—a sort of dragon with large head, gaping mouth, and short legs—similarly mounted; the fourth slab, on the south-west, has a man with a shield, mounted on the shoulder of a larger human figure which seems to have borne a female figure on his left shoulder, but she is seriously damaged. The next, on the south-east, has the animal so destroyed that it is doubtful what it was; and the last appears to have been a ram, similarly mounted.

The pendentive in the centre of the dome has been boldly designed and well executed, but is damaged at the point. It hangs from a circle 7 feet 10 inches in diameter, and the point is 12 feet 10 inches from the raised circular flagstone, which is 4 inches above the floor. The dome springs at a height of 11 feet 1 inch from the floor. (See photograph, Plate VI.)

The photograph, Plate III, shows the style of the roof to have been Draviḍian: this was overgrown with grass when Col. Biggs' photograph of this temple was taken, and he seems to have made no notes. His photograph also shewed only the front manḍap of the temple. From the similarity of its pillars to those of the Nandi Pavilion at Halabid,

PLATE V.

BELGÂM - INNER DOOR OF TEMPLE No. II.

PLATE VI.

BELGÂM - CEILING OF JAINA TEMPLE No. II.

2

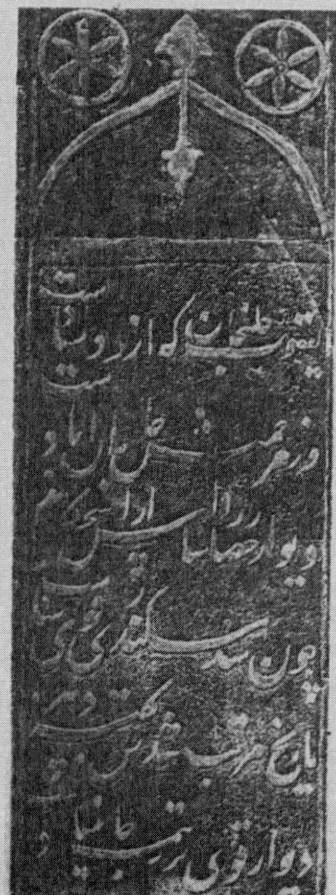

Size, 3 ft. 2 in. by 1 ft. 1 in.

1

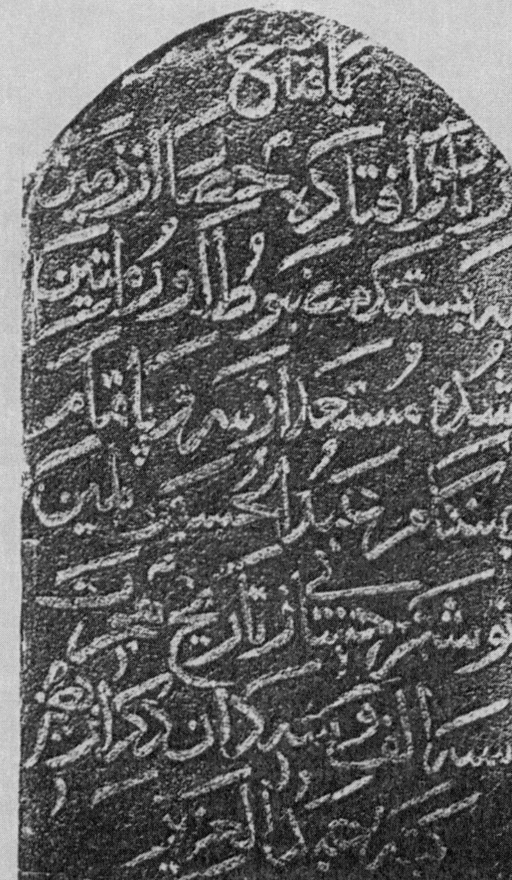

Size, 2 ft. 4 in. by 1 ft. 4 in.

4

Size, 2 ft. 2 in. by 1 ft.

3

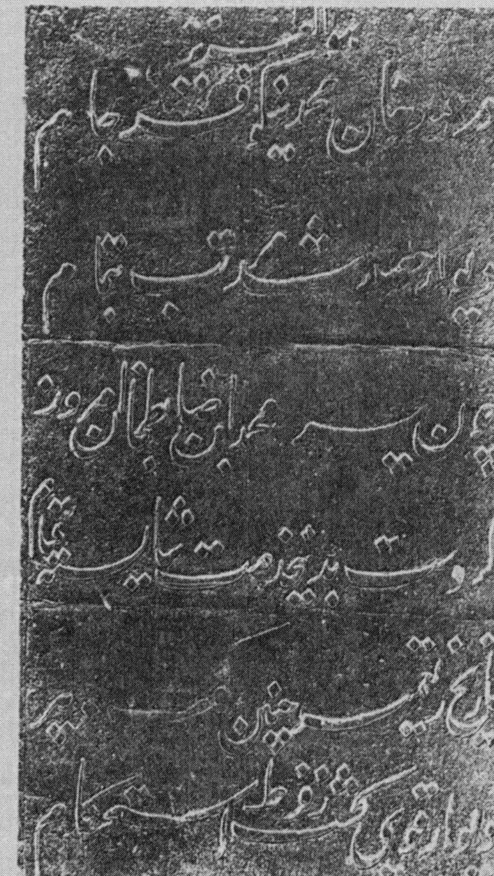

Size, 2 ft. 8 in. by 1 ft. 6 in.

Mr. Fergusson relegated it* with remarkable precision to the twelfth and thirteenth centuries, and we now find it belongs to the beginning of the thirteenth; "its cornices" as he remarked, "of Dravidian outline indicate that if so, it was erected by a people more influenced by southern feelings than the Bellalas; and the principal point of interest (in Col. Biggs' photograph) is the clearness with which it illustrates the construction of these cornices. The mode by which they were clipped under the first cornice of the roof and the upper side of the architrave is clearly seen in the photograph, as also the horizontal bracket by which the outer edge was supported. On the longer faces this seems to have been constructively sufficient; but at the angle of the clip or hold under the roof does not seem to have sufficed, and the angle stones have consequently in nearly every instance fallen away."

The temples are both in the same style, though very different in plan and detail. In the śikhar or spire above the second is a small square chamber, such as is common in Jaina temples for a secondary image.

The only inscriptions now in the Fort are in the Persian character, and copies of all except one on the Masjid were taken. One on the north-east wall (Plate VII. No. 1.) in a recess in the parapet runs thus,—

"Ya'qûb 'Alî Khân, who is a joy to the heart, and by whose benevolence the "world is prosperous, built the wall of the citadel strengthening it with a strong founda- "tion like the wall of Alexander." The chronogram gives the date A. Hijrah 937, or 1530 A.D.

Another inscription in the south-east part of the Fort (No. 2) relates to the rebuilding of a portion of the wall in that quarter in A.H. 1043 or A.D. 1633–34. I sent a tracing of this inscription to Professor Blochmann of Calcutta who returns the following reading and translation :—

یا فتاح
ذباداں فتادہ حصار از زمین
بہ بستند مضبوط اورا متین
شدہ مستعد از سروپا تمام
بہنگام عبد الحسین مکین
نوشتہ حسابي ز تاریخ ھجرت
سنہ الف وسہ داں در اربعین
کتبہ عبد العزیز

O Opener! The Fort having been destroyed by the rains, it was again made strong and firm. It was entirely renovated in the time of 'Abdul Husain, the powerful. A reckoning according to the date of the Hijrah was written down: know it to be the year 1043. *Written by 'Abdul 'Aziz.*

The metre is *Mutaqârib;* but the 5th hemistich alone is *sâlim.*

Copies—or rather "estampages"—were made of Nos. 3 and 4 (Plate VIII.), and are given in reduced facsimile. No. 3 is built into the front wall of the library, which was formerly the Kiledâr's house. It is dated 1648, and states that in the time of Khân Muhammad, the fort wall was completed by Muhammad bin Zabit Khân. "Who the "latter is," says Mr. H. J. Stokes, M.C.S.,† "I cannot ascertain, but Muhammad Khân "was a conspicuous officer in the Bîjâpur army of that time, in whose jâghîr Belgâm "was probably included."

---

* *Architecture of Dharwar and Mysore*, p. 59.

† *Selections from the Records of the Bombay Government*, No. cxv. p. 40.

A photograph was taken of the north gate of the fort, from the inside, which, with its great lintel, and guard-house affords a good example of the Muhammadan style in these provinces in the fifteenth and sixteenth centuries.

Konur.

On 7th February, the work at Belgâm was concluded and on the morning of Monday 9th, we started for Ankalgi monastery. We next moved to Gokâk, but could hear of no Buddhist remains (as rumoured)* in the vicinity, and we proceeded next day to Konur. There are some śilaśâśanams here, but I did not attempt to copy them, nor an inscription on a carved stone in a ruinous temple on the outskirts of the village; but took a photograph of what remains of a fine old temple, the maṇḍap of which is entirely gone.

About a mile from the village of Konur are the falls—usually known as the Falls of Gokâk,—where the Ghâṭprabhâ river plunges over a perpendicular rock 180 feet in height, and of great width during the rains. Just opposite to this splendid cataract, on each side of the river, temples have been erected at an early date. The earliest erections have probably entirely disappeared, and even of those from the ninth till the twelfth or thirteenth century there are only fragments left on the steep slope of the north bank of the river, overgrown by prickly pear and thorny shrubs.

The large temple of Mahâlingeśvara (Plates IX. and X.) on the south side is generally speaking a very plain structure, built of large stones, with flat ceilings, Four pillars in the centre of the maṇḍap have square bases, octagon mouldings, then a square plain block, round neck and capital, with square abacus. The pillars of the porches have mostly round smooth shafts. In the east porch is a long inscription in ancient characters, but so besmeared with paint that portions of it are quite illegible. Such as it is, a photograph of it was taken with some difficulty. It appears to be much older than the temple, and was probably removed from some of the neighbouring buildings now in ruins.

The columns are 8 feet 9 inches high, exclusive of the brackets; the screen is 3 feet 3 inches high inside, with a ledge outside the line of the pillars. The door into the antechamber has a perforated panel on each side. There are Śaiva dwârpâlas or door-keepers on the jambs, each with four hands, and holding the *triśula* or trident, and *damru* or small drum of Śiva. Two smaller ones have the mace and fruit; and on the walls, behind them, on the right is Kârttikeya, and on the left, perhaps, Brahmâ, with a mace in his right hand. The door of the shrine is very plain. The back of the maṇḍap has been repaired since the temple was originally built.

The brackets of the capitals have the cobra ornament, as at Belgâm. The outside of the roof is much ruined, but the style has been Draviḍian.

On the east side, opposite the shrine, is another temple, with four square columns inside, of a rather antique pattern, and four perfectly plain shafts in front,—which must have formed the pilasters in the wall. Behind the second pair of columns, at the entrance to an open fronted antechamber to the shrine, are two of the

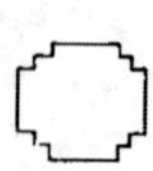

usual broken-square form. The door to the shrine is somewhat elaborately carved, with two male and two female figures below on the jambs. On the step are two conch shells forming the buds of a flower, as in the Jaina temples of Neminâtha and in Vaishṇava temples. The shrine contains a *linga;*

* *Jour. Bomb. B. R. Asiat. Soc.* Vol. III. pt. ii. p. 61.

PLATE IX.

TEMPLE OF MAHÂLINGEŚVARA NEAR KONUR.

TEMPLE OF MAHÂLINGEŚVARA NEAR KONUR. PLATE X.

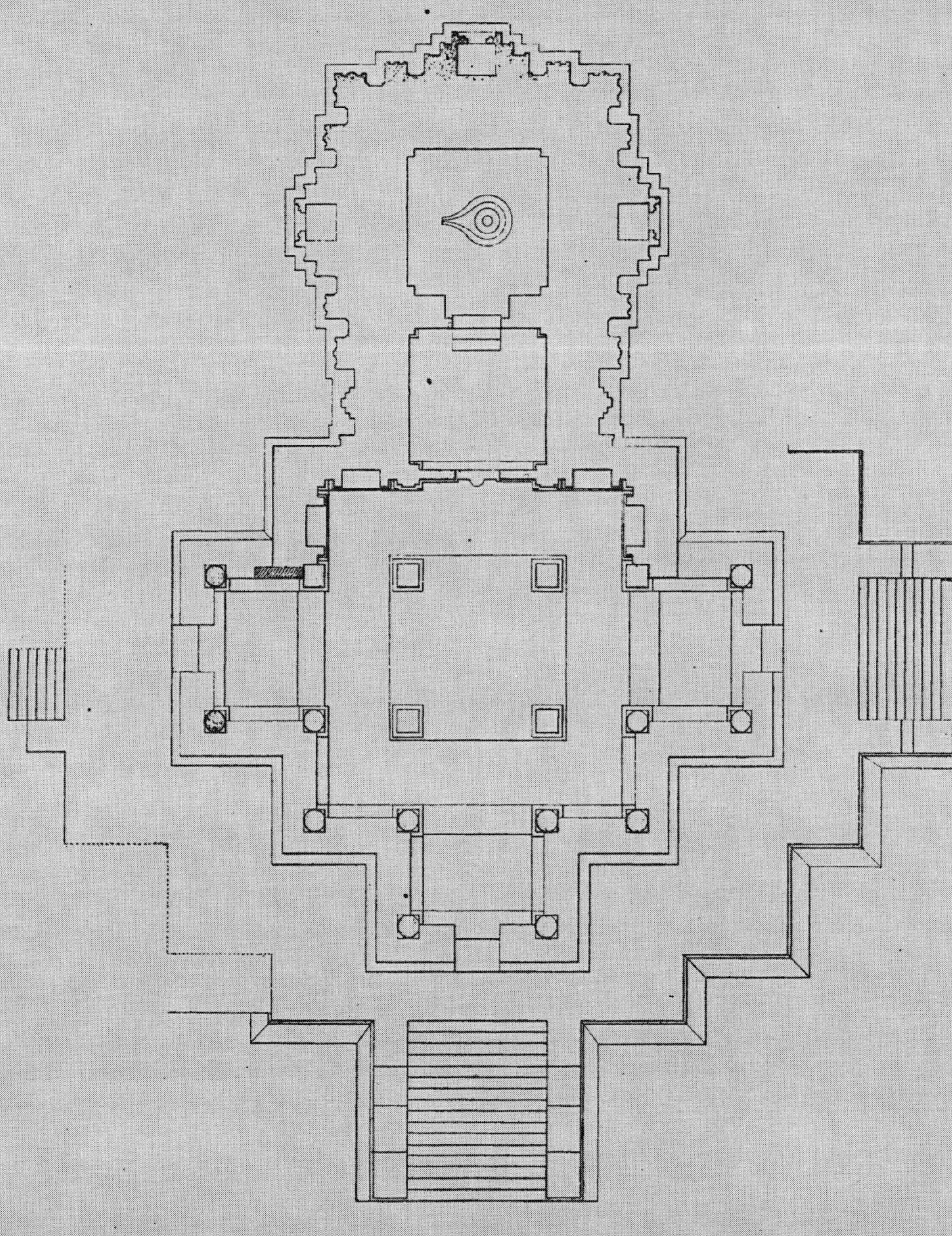

J. Burgess, delt.

behind the door are large holes for an enormous bar; and the walls are of great thickness. On the east side is a shelf, and below it is the water conduit. The pillars are all single blocks, and this temple seems considerably older than that now in use.

Behind this last is a small shrine facing east, with antechamber and porch, about 6 feet high inside. The door of the shrine is tastefully carved, and bears a Gaṇapati on the lintel,—the usual cognizance of a Śaiva temple. The pillars are square, and the outside walls are fallen away.

South of this last, and facing north, is another shrine which appears to be very old. It has four pillars in the floor, and a verandah with pilasters and two columns in antis. Altogether, it is the pattern of a Buddhist cave, and, though the walls have been rebuilt in more recent times, it is perhaps a fragment of one of the earliest temples here. The door is peculiarly like the cave pattern.

West of this is a neat little temple, ruined in front, with four columns inside the maṇḍap, of the same style as the great temple, but more elegant. On the screen are four square columns and two pilasters. The antechamber has two smaller pillars in front, like some of the caves. The shrine door is very neat, but without animal representation. The snake is represented on the brackets of the pillars. The floors of the shrine and antechamber have been recently dug up in search of treasure. This temple is, perhaps, the most modern here.

To the west of the great temple is the shrine and antechamber of another, very similar to the large one, but on a smaller scale.

On the opposite or north side of the river is—*first*, a small temple, of which only the shrine and entrance to it are nearly entire. Over the porch or antechamber to the shrine is a carved slab, in the centre of which is Kâlî with a crooked sword,

heavy earrings, a heavy chain over the brow and in place of the usual necklace of skulls; in her eight hands she holds a shield, a human head, a mace or sceptre, &c. At her left foot is a figure on a dog, at the right another beating a drum. In the next compartment, nearer the shrine, is a dancing *Devî* with four arms, and smaller figures on each side. In the corner compartment to the right is Gaṇapati. On the right side compartment, is a female with a strap across the bosom, seizing a smaller female by the hair; below is a dog and a sheep. In the front compartments are three dancing females, one with a strap across the breasts; and with these are other smaller figures in the same compartments. On the east side compartment is Varâha,—the boar-headed incarnation of Vishṇu, with large breasts, a small figure on an animal, &c.; and in the last (corner) compartment is a dancing *devî*, with four arms, strap and small figures below. On the lintel is Śiva and Pârvatî (or possibly Vishṇu and Lakshmî) seated on his knee. Loose slabs lie about, representing the same pair, Brahma (or Śiva) with three faces, &c. May this small temple in this wild and sequestered spot not have witnessed the demoniac orgies and the revolting sacrifice so vividly pourtrayed in the *Mâlatimâdhava?* (See Wilson's *Hindu Theatre.*)

Second.—Higher up the hill are fragments of four other temples of the same style, entirely ruined. Beside them is a much larger one, surrounded by prickly pear and partially filled with earth, and so infested by bats as to be almost unenterable. The pillars are square, like those of the older temple on the north side, but the torus of the capital is circular. It has been a triple temple, facing south, and directly opposite the larger temple on the other side, with the falls in a line between. Farther east is a smaller one, not over six feet high, with four plain columns in the hall, and pilasters with two columns in antis in front. The antechamber and shrine are small, and the walls are thin, being formed of large slabs set on edge. There are no sculptures to indicate its character.

West of these is a fragment of another, about five feet high, quite plain, with two square pillars.

To the south-east of Konur are the remains of a large number of dolmens. They are scattered over a considerable area, but have recently suffered grievously at the hands of the *Wadárís*,* or wandering navvies.

A little to the south-east of the village is the first group, in which one remains entire, standing beside a heap of small stones, with which it was doubtless at one time covered. The capstone is a conglomerate slab about a foot thick, 8 feet long, and of varying breadth from 4 feet 2 inches to 8 feet. This rests on five stones,—two side stones about 4½ feet long by 3 feet 8 inches high, a back 4 feet 3 inches long, and two stones in front about 2 feet long each. The cell is thus 2 feet 9 inches wide in front, 4 feet 3 inches at the back, and about 4 feet in length. The entrance between the front stones is 18 inches wide, and from the entrance two lower stones extend outwards about 5½ feet, forming a sort of alley or passage up to the entrance. Other examples shew that this was a low-covered passage, by which the inner cell could be reached, when the whole was covered over with small stones as a sort of cairn. One, beside this one, is said to have been excavated by some European, and to have yielded ashes, bones, and earthenware pottery. To the south-west of this there crop through the sand one or two large slabs, probably the capstones of as yet undisturbed dolmens; but, unless prevented by the authorities, it is not likely the Wadâris will long leave them undestroyed. The entrances to the south are a little to the west of it.

Across two fields to the south-east is a still larger collection, of which five or six still retain their capstones; others have them broken; two are apparently unopened; and in two cases the stones over the entrances still remain *in situ*, shewing that they were covered passages. Thirty or forty here have been ruined. All are surrounded by loose stones, with which they have at one time been covered, and one or two mounds may possibly be undisturbed ones. One is 5 feet 9 inches high inside, 4 feet 8 inches wide at the back, 5 feet 10 inches long, and 2 feet wide in front; and the entrance must have been 2½ feet high. (See photograph, Plate XI.)

On the west side of the road is one with the capstone, but one of the front stones is removed and the east side one broken; the front is undisturbed, and part of the cairn or mound still rests against the south-east side. To the south are fragments of three others.

Still farther west are twenty to twenty-five others; three of them with capstones, one just chipped, and a fifth that must have been smashed up by Wadâris very shortly before my examination of them. One or two capstones just show above ground here.

---

* See *Indian Antiquary*, Vol. III. p. 185.

DOLMEN AT KONUR.

KÂDAROḶI - OLD TEMPLE IN THE BED OF THE MÂLAPRABHÂ RIVER.

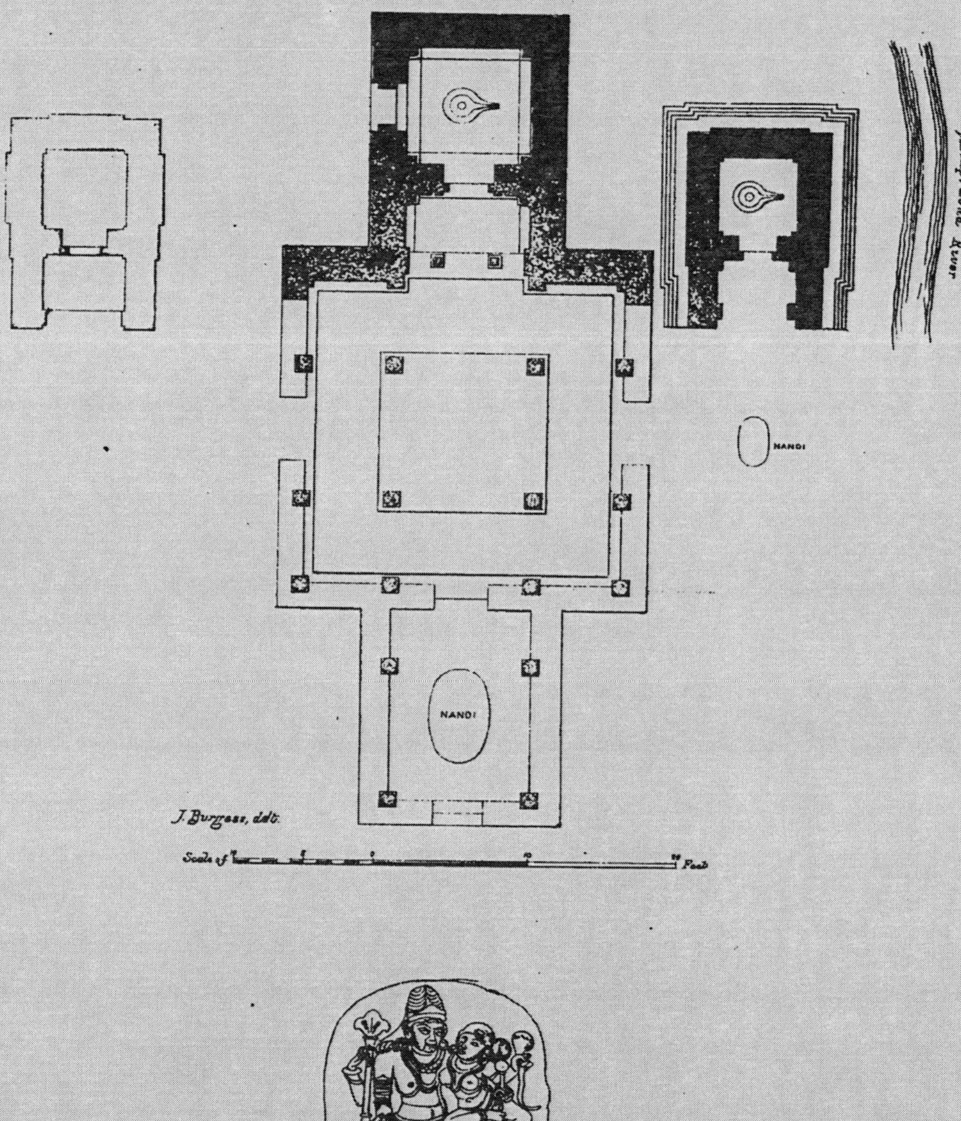

From Konur I proceeded to Hukeri, where are some Muhammadan tombs and mosques of the early half of the sixteenth century; but they are much scattered and did not seem deserving of the time necessary to plan and photograph them. Leaving this, we made a march of 18 miles to Sutgati, which was reached in the evening of 17th Feb. Next day we reached Belgâm, and spent Thursday in getting ready to march eastwards.

Kâdaroḷi.

On Friday evening we arrived at Kâdaroḷi, anciently Kâdaravaḷḷi, on the river Mâlaprabhâ, where is a curious old temple of Śankaradeva, built of black stone, in the bed of the river, which must be quite inaccessible during floods. The temple, or temples—for there are three shrines—appear to have always been Śaiva; but, as is frequently the case in these districts, there are Vaishṇava sculptures lying about, which may have been placed in the maṇḍap when it was entire. Nothing but the shrines and their antechambers now remain entire: the central shrine is 8 feet 3⅓ inches square, and each of the side ones 5 feet 6½ inches. The pillars of the maṇḍap and portico to the central temple, with the low screen wall that surrounded them, also remain; but the roofs and the capitals of all the columns have been carried off, in all probability by the river. See plan, Plate XII. fig. 1. Fig. 2 is a sketch of Śankaradeva or Śiva with his consort Pârvatî, from a slab in the temple.

There is no inscription on the temple, except a few letters on one of the pillars and on an old loose image of Gaṇapati; but in the verandah of a temple in the modern village, is a *śilaśâsana* or stone tablet, about twenty inches broad and five and a half feet high, Plate XIII. It stood originally in front of this temple in the river, where, owing to its submergence during the rains, it was every year becoming further buried in the ground. Mr. J. F. Fleet, Bo.C.S. accordingly had it removed to the village of Kâdaroḷi, where it now is.

The slab bears at the top,—in the centre a Linga or phallic emblem of Śiva on its *chavaranga* or altar-pedestal, with a priest officiating at it; to the left is a figure of the bull Nandi or Basava couching, with the sun above it; and to the right a cow and calf, with the moon above them. The average length of the lines is from 18 to 19½ inches, and the letters are old Kanarese excellently preserved. The language is almost entirely Sanskṛit, but the idiom and inflections are old Kanarese.

The following translation of it was made by Mr. Fleet: *—

Translation.

Reverence to Śambhu, the foundation-pillar for the erection of the city of the three worlds, who is resplendent with his *chaunri*, which is the moon that kisses his lofty head.

Hail! While the victorious rule of the fortunate Bhuvanaikamalladeva,—the asylum of the whole world, the favourite of the earth, the great king of kings, the supreme lord, the most venerable, the forehead-ornament of the Satyâśrayakuḷa, the glory of the Châlukyas,—was flourishing with perpetual increase so as to endure as long as the moon and sun and stars might last, he who flourished on the lotuses that were his feet (*was*)—the fortunate prime minister Someśvarabhaṭṭa, the chief of the houses of Heri, Sandhi, and Vigrahi, the commander of the forces, who was possessed

* Conf. *Indian Antiquary*, Vol. I. p. 141.

of all the glory of the names of—"The great chief of chieftains who has attained the "five great śabdas,* the bold Daṇḍanâyaka (*commander of troops*) the conferrer of "happiness on good people, he who abounds in fame, he whose ornament is the welfare "of others, (*or* who labours for the good of others), the moon of the ocean of affability, "he who abounds in the quality of bravery, he who restrains the fury of his foes, "Naṇṇana-(*or* Aṇṇana-)gandhavâraṇa,"—and others also.

At his command, the fortunate commander of the forces, Keśavâdityadeva possessed of all the glory of the names of—"The great chief of chieftains, who has "attained the five great śabdas, the bold Daṇḍanâyaka, he who confers boons upon "Brahmans, he who is pure of lineage, the best friend of good people, the grantor of all "the desires of his relations, the crest-jewel of good people, he who is terrible to the "forces of his foes, he who is a very mine for the jewel of truth, the impetuous Mâva-"nasinga," and others,—in the year of the Śaka era 997, being the Râkshasasam-vatsara, at the moment of the conjunction of a vyatipâta with the sun's commencement of his northward progress, on Sunday, the day of the full moon of Pushya,†—gave as a yearly grant five golden gadyâṇas of Gaṅga in (*out of*) the customs of Vaḍḍarâvaḷa,‡ for the purposes of the *angabhoga* § of the god Śankaradeva of Kâdaravaḷḷi.

Whosoever preserves this act of piety, his reward is as great as if he had, at Vâra-ṇâsi, or at Prayâge, at Arghyatîrtha, or at Kurukshetra, fashioned out of the five jewels the horns and hoofs of twelve thousand cows of a tawny colour, and given to Brahmans who are well versed in the Vedas the gift called *Ubhayamukhîdâna*.‖ But he who destroys this act of piety commits a sin as great as if, at those same holy places, he had destroyed the same number of tawny cows.

He who appropriates land that has been bestowed either by himself or by another is born for sixty thousand years as a worm in ordure. "This general bridge of piety, "which belongs in common to all rulers of mankind, should at all times be preserved "by you,"—thus does Râmachandra makes his earnest request to all future kings.

This is the writing of Singoja, the son of Samboja, a very bee at the lotuses which are the feet of the god Śankaradeva. May the greatest prosperity attend it!

This inscription then refers to a certain gift or yearly grant by Keśavâdityadeva, the commander-in-chief of the Kâlyâṇi sovereign Someśvara Deva II., known as Bhuvanaikamalladeva, in the Śaka year 997, or A.D. 1075;—that is about a year before he was dethroned by his brother Tribhuvanamalla or Vikramâditya VI. Bhuvanaikamalla was the successor of Âhavamalla or Someśvara Deva I., who must have begun to reign about A.D. 1040, and whom Sir W. Elliott supposes to have died about A.D. 1069: he seems from an inscription at Ḍambaḷ¶ to have been alive at least in 1062 A.D. This Châlukya dynasty, which was restored in the person of

---

* "It is usual," says Mr. Shankar P. Pandit, "to render this to mean 'who has obtained the five great sounds,' viz., of certain musical instruments. But it seems more probable that *mahâśabda* refers to certain five *titles*, though I am not certain what these titles were. The word *mahâśabda* appears to refer to five words or titles beginning with *mahâ*, such as Mahârajâ, Mahâmaṇḍaleśvara," &c.—*Ind. Antiquary*, Vol. I. p. 81, note.

† About the end of January, 1075, A.D.

‡ It is not clear whether this is the name of a locality or the name of a particular tax.

§ The decoration of the image of the god with clothes, ornaments, &c.

‖ Literally "the gift of (*a cow*) that has two faces;" the ceremony is performed by fashioning out of the five jewels, a diamond, a pearl, a sapphire, an emerald, and a piece of coral, the image of a cow in the act of bringing forth a calf, when, of course, there are two heads to apparently only one body, and presenting it to a Brahman.

¶ See *Ind. Antiquary*, Vol. II. p. 297, and conf. Vol. III. p. 89.

SAMPGÂṄW - PLAN OF THE MOSQUE. PLATE XIV.

1. PLAN

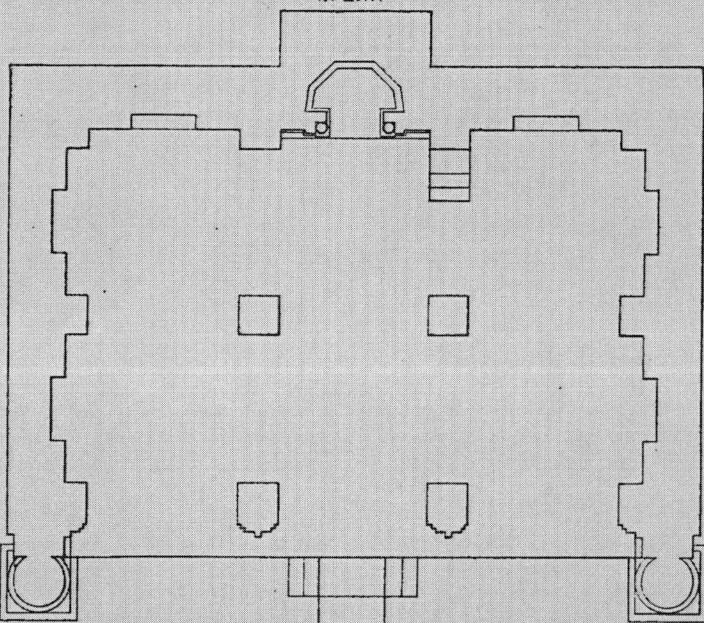

2

INSCRIPTION 6.

BAIL-HANGAL - PLAN OF THE OLD TEMPLE.

3. PLAN

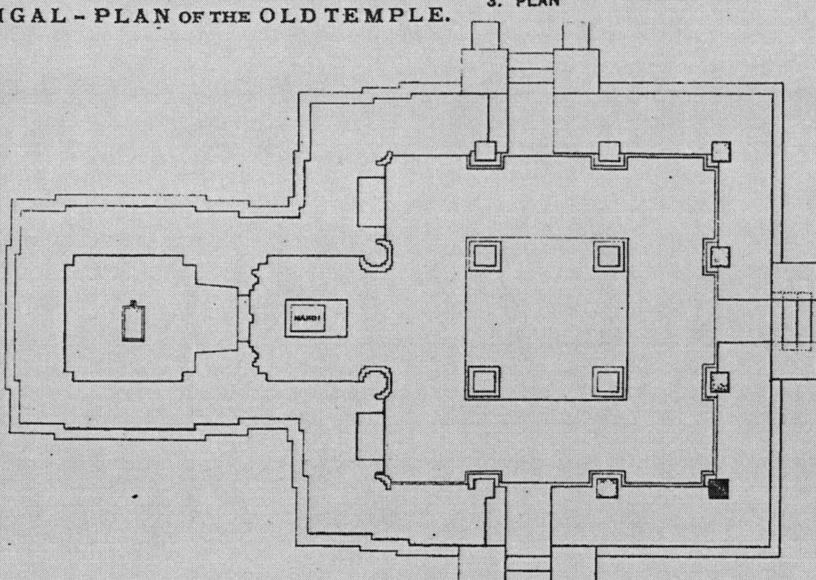

J. Burgess, delt.

Scale of Feet

Tailabhûpa in A.D. 973, was originally founded in A.D. 609 by Satyâśraya, one of the sons of Kîrttivarma, and from him took the title of Satyâśrayakûla, as in this inscription. This temple was therefore an established shrine in the latter part of the eleventh century; how long *before* that time we know not. It is so unlike any other that I have yet met with, that it would be hazardous to venture an opinion respecting its age; but I am inclined to think it belongs to about the ninth century,—possibly earlier. A large fragment of another *śilaśâsana*, quite uncared for, lies in the village, which, if decipherable, might possibly throw some further light on the history of the place.

Sampgâṅw and Bail-Hangal.

On Monday 23rd Feb. we started at 4 a.m. and walked to Sampgâṅw on foot. The Masjid here is rather low in the roof, otherwise the building is well proportioned and pleasing. A photograph was taken of it and a ground plan (Plate XIV. fig. 1). Over the *mihrab* is the inscription, of which the accompanying copy (Plate XIV. 2) is reduced from a rubbing. It contains no historical information, however; only three verses from the Qorân, *viz.*, sûrah lxi. 13, xii. 64, and vi. 161. In the afternoon, the luggage and a tent were sent ahead to Bail-Hangal, which we reached at 11.30 p.m., before the tent was pitched.

The temple of Bail-Hangal may date from about A.D. 1200. A small Gaṇapati over the shrine door, and its present dedication to the *linga*, would indicate a Śaiva origin; but few old Śaiva temples in this part of the country have Gaṇapati in this position, and the Jaina look of the place makes it suspicious whether it has not been appropriated by the Lingayats. A photograph was taken of the front of the temple and a ground plan (Plate XIV. fig. 3). An inscription on a large stone slab in front of this temple is much weatherworn, and ought to be removed to a less exposed place. Another inscription, in a ditch close by, I did not discover till too late to examine.

Saundati and Yellamâ.

25th February. We started at 6 a.m. and reached Gurlâ Husur at 11 a.m. Finding nothing of note here, I proceeded in the evening, and reached Saundati at 9 p.m. In the Fort here, built by the Deśai of Nurgund, there is a temple of Bhavânî. I visited all the temples in the village, but they are in a very ruinous and patched condition, and did not seem likely to repay any careful examination. In the Kacheri are two inscriptions, removed thither by Mr. Stokes: the larger, and complete, one was photographed. It consists of ninety-three lines, in Kanarese mixed with Sanskrit, and had been previously taken by Major Biggs. It was analysed by the late Dr. Bhâu Dâjî as follows:—"The name Mallikârjuna is frequently met with, and may be the name of a king. Lakshmî-deva of the Ratta Kula, is praised. In the fifth line the Ratta dynasty and descendants of the Râshṭra Kûta dynasty are mentioned. Lakshmî-deva does not appear to have been a king, but probably a minister or high officer. Kuṇḍi-deśa is mentioned. The name of a *Râja-guru* or Royal Guide—Munichandra, is read: he was probably of the Jaina faith. Mallikârjuṇa appears in some places to be the name of the king or minister, whilst in others it appears to refer to the great shrine of Mallikârjuna. In one place (the eleventh line) he is called a son of Kâma Râja; in another place Sâmâsiga; his wife's name was Gaurî: he lived at Kolâra. His guru (spiritual adviser) was Munichandra. By his direction the god Mallinâtha was established (*in a temple*). There are several names of Munis, such as Śrî Munivari, Muni Mukhya, Kânteya, Suyyapatî, Vrate, Valuvarmâ, and Samkama. Next follows the praise of the poet Rudra-bhaṭṭa. In the sixty-first line a second story commences with Lakshmî-deva, who had the five great titles* and is styled Mahâmandaleśvara Lattana puravarâdhiśvara Ratta-kula bhûshaṇa Sindhura Lânchhana Sushviśadayaso Lânchhana Suvarṇa garuda dhvaja Sâhasottunga, &c. He lived in Venugrâma. The inscription was written in the Śaka year 1151 (A.D. 1229). By the direction of Râja-guru Munichandra, a village called Nirvali was given for the support of the temple of Mallinâtha. The sixty-ninth line concludes this portion: then follows another inscription. The grantor is Keśi-Râja to Mallinâtha. Matîmâ-deva, Gahâlya Mânikya, Basadiyâchârya, Prabhâchandra, Siddhântideva, Subhachandra, Siddhântideva Sipparappa, Indrakîrti-deva, Śrî Dhara-deva, and other names occur; some of them ending in *chandra*, appear to belong to the Diagmbara Jainas."†

This inscription, only twenty-four years later than that of Belgâm, and by a prince residing also at Venugrâma, probably relates to the same dynasty—the Rattas; and it is not improbable that the Lakshmî-bhupati of the one may prove to be the Lakshmî-deva of the other, and the Mallikârjuna mentioned in both, the same person. A critical version of both these inscriptions, and of any others that may be found relating to the Ratta dynasty is much desiderated. They were evidently great patrons of the Jainas; and this grant is to a temple of Mallinâtha, the nineteenth of their Tîrthañkaras or Jinas.

At 4 p.m. we were on the way to Yellamâ. This shrine is famous throughout the Kanarese districts. It is built in the bed of the Sarasvatî, a small stream running eastwards from the hills above Saundati. The temple—said to be 2000 years old—in its present form has been rebuilt, except perhaps the shrine, within the last century or two, and its predecessor did not probably date from before the commencement of the thirteenth century. It stands in the middle of a court surrounded by arcades with pointed arches. In the west gate are some pillars similar to those of the Jaina temples at Belgâm, and on the base of one is an inscription covered with whitewash; and at a small shrine of Gaṇapati to the north are two rough pillars, one with an inscription of 11¼ lines in Kanarese. There had been very heavy rains a few days previously, and the roads were much cut up by it. At 6.45 a.m. next morning we started for Huli.

Huli.

The large temple of Panchalinga (photograph, Plate XV.) at Huli has been erected by Jainas: it consists of a large outer maṇdap, an inner one, 41 feet 9 inches in length, with a triple shrine at the back and one at each end, as shewn in the plan, Plate XVI. The Jinas have been hewn off all the lintels except that over the entrance to the shrine at the south end, which has the finest door. The temple faces the East.

* Vide ante, p. 9, note.

† *Jour. Bom. B.R. As. Soc.*, Vol. IX. p. 324.

HULI-TEMPLE OF PANCHALINGA DEVA.

HULI-TEMPLE OF PANCHALINGADEVA. PLATE XVI.

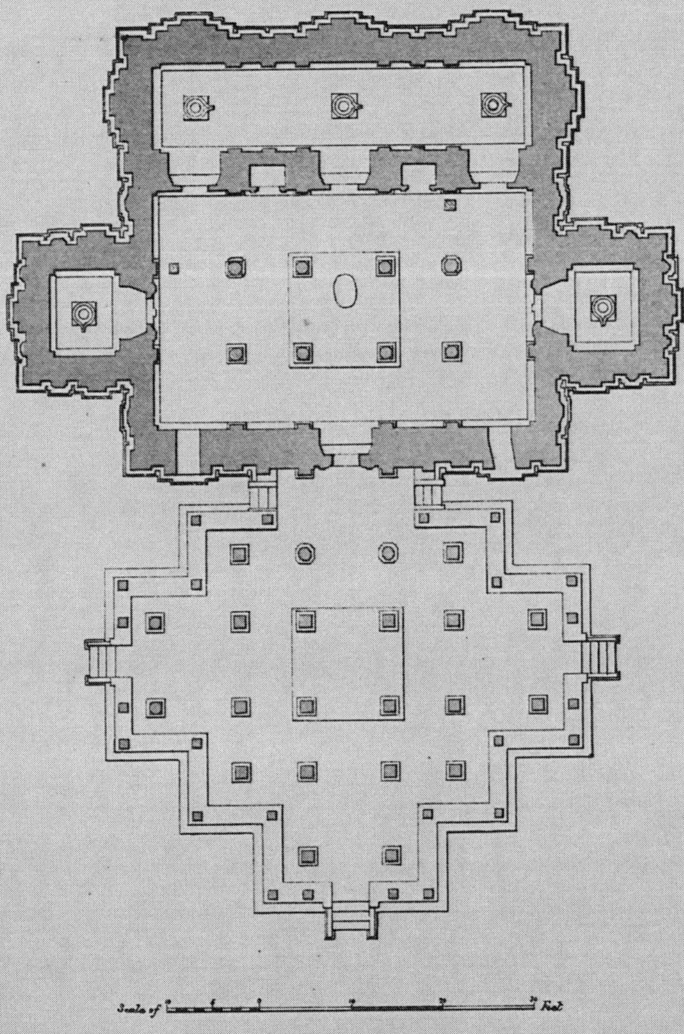

J. Burgess, delt.

On two pillars of the outer maṇḍap are Kanarese inscriptions, probably cut when the temple was appropriated by the Lingayats. One of them begins :—

[illegible]

[illegible]

[illegible]

There are four or five different styles of columns, symmetrically arranged in the maṇḍap. Except lotuses carved in five or six compartments, the roofs are plain. The temple probably belongs to about the year 1100 A.D. Two photographs were taken of it, from the east and north.

At the foot of the hill to the north of the village is a group of temples in ruins, probably of about the same age. One of these, built of hard, compact, bluish stone, has a maṇḍap about 43 feet from north to south. The four central pillars are similar to those at Belgâm, only the snake is wanting on the bracket. The short pillars on the screen are of considerable variety of pattern—hexagonal, octagonal, and circular. The door f the shrine is of porphyry richly carved: and n the lintel is Śrî or Lakshmî with elephants ouring water over her—a very common emblem n the temples in these districts. As this symol is of so frequent occurrence, the accompanyng woodcut is borrowed from Fergusson's *Tree nd Serpent Worship* (p. 108) to illustrate it.)f course the details vary in different sculptures: n some, the *chauṅri*-bearers below the elephants re entirely wanting, and the elephants are nade larger and not raised so much above the ead of the Devî as represented here. It is urious to remark how early this figure appears n Indian sculpture: a form of it is found in the arly Buddhist caves at Udayagiri in Orissa, and epresented in Fergusson's *Tree and Serpent Vorship*, Plate C. fig. 3. She also appears frequently on the gates of the Sâṅchi Tope,* and, s the goddess of riches and good fortune, is favourite with the Jainas, and invoked in their nscriptions. Outside, the walls of the shrine are in ruins.

Śrî Consort of Vishṇu.

From an image brought from Indore, engraved in Moor's Pantheon, Plate 30.

Standing against the ruins of an old temple close by, is a large inscription in good preservation; and all around are fragments of buildings with pillars of the plainest and roughest style, slabs of granite and porphyry, carved stones, pieces of inscriptions, &c.

---

* *Tree and Serpent Worship*, 2nd Ed., pp. 112, 113, 120, 242, 268.

Below this is a tank, and on the north side of it is a temple having an inscription in the west wall, with a figure of Vishṇu on Śeshnâga—suspiciously like as if carved after the inscription, in substitution for something else. Over the shrine door is Lakshmî and the elephants.

On the west side of the tank are several shrines which were photographed. The most southerly is only the antechamber and shrine of a temple, with a standing figure on the lintel of the door. The next has a highly carved door, with Lakshmî and the elephants on the lintel and dancing figures down the jambs. Two pillars of the maṇḍap are still standing. To the north of this again is another with six pillars of the maṇḍap still left. Round their bases have been figures carved in high relief—as at Ambarnâth, but they are now defaced. Round the necks of these columns are solid iron rings. The antechamber has had two small pillars in front—one is still standing, and there appears to have been at one time a screen between the middle pair. The roofs are flat, except that there is a lotus over the centre of the maṇḍap and of the antechamber. There are two niches, in which there were probably inscriptions, but they are now gone. This temple bears very evident marks of having been wilfully destroyed.

To the west of these, overgrown by prickly pear, is an old shrine with a small open maṇḍap: the door from this to the inner and larger one is richly carved with a wonderful variety of Nâgas and Nâginîs intertwined in every variety of ways. The inner *shâla,* of four columns, has an antechamber with two small columns in front, and another richly carved door leads to the shrine. Over both doors is Lakshmî with the elephants,—shewing that it was a Vaishṇava temple.

North-west from this is a small modern shrine with a remarkable snake figure in the area. The shrine itself, inside, was perhaps originally Jaina, with old looking pillars; but Lakshmî is now carved on the lintel. There are carved slabs lying about and built into the surrounding wall,—some, in a slaty stone, are carved with great spirit,—mostly Vaishṇava in subject.

All around Huli there are enough carved stones to furnish a museum or illustrate a mythology. Were there a provincial museum at Belgâm, as there ought to be, abundant materials might be found here to furnish it. From the *débris* of all sorts, the walls and foundations of grey granite, the inscriptions, and sculptured stones, that lie scattered about Huli and the vicinity, it would seem as if it had at one time been a great *tîrtha,* probably at first Buddhist or early Jaina, and appropriated afterwards by Vaishṇavas and Smârttas.

East-south-east from the tank above mentioned, on a mound that must have been on the bank of a large artificial lake, is another temple,—its maṇḍap much dilapidated. Outside it is a plain structure, and the door of the antechamber to the shrine is quite plain; but that of the shrine has lines of dancers and *Nâga* figures round it, Lakshmî with elephants and trees on the lintel, and over her, some Deva. The walls are of great thickness,—the slabs set on edge. The pillars that support the maṇḍap are much plainer than the rest of the temple. Inside is a Lingayat inscription, a curious Nâga figure, and a Gaṇapati—probably brought from some other temple.

Sinde-Manauli.

2nd March.—Outside the village of Manauli, and in an enclosure surrounded by a high wall, are the temples of Panchalinga Deva—eight in all, two very small, and two

PLATE XVII.

BADÂMI - FRONT OF CAVE I.

larger than the rest. One of the latter is a triple temple and Jaina in style. On the lintel of the doorway of one of the others is Lakshmî with the elephants. The other large one facing the east is regarded as the principal temple here, is jealously guarded, and has an outer open maṇḍap and an inner closed one—without window. In the outer are several carved stones, a number of which were grouped together and photographed, as was also a large inscription outside.

These temples are of coarse grained stone, no way remarkable for carving, and they have been repaired and whitewashed over and over again till they look vulgar in the extreme. The snake head on the bracket, and the general style of them, would lead us to assign them to about the same age as the Belgâm temples, or the end of the twelfth century, possibly a little older. The triple temple is entire except the spires, and its three antechambers to the shrines lead off from the inner or closed maṇḍap. The roofs are now flat, and a clumsy lion is placed over the front or north face.

Badâmi.

From Manauli I made two marches to Badâmi. On the north-east of the town is the fort, on the outskirts of which are some temples. On the south is another rocky hill, also formerly fortified. It is in this hill that the cave temples are: three of them Brahmanical and the fourth Jaina. There is also a cave formed by a large mass of rock that has fallen down, near the east end of the large tank, on the east of the town, between the two forts. The entrance is by a hole through which one may crawl in. Against the rock at the back is a large figure of a Jina, and another smaller one—otherwise there is no carving about this cave: no attempt has been made even to make it more regular in shape or height. Among the ignorant villagers the Jina is regarded as the image of the Râja who formed the beautiful tank or lake between this spot and the village.

The Caves will be best understood from the drawings. They stand, as to arrangement of parts, between the Buddhist Vihâras and the later Brahmanical examples at Elora, Elephanta, and Salsette. The front wall of the Buddhist vihâra with its small windows and doors admitted too little light; and so, here, while retaining the verandah in front, and further protecting the cave from rain and sun by projecting eaves, the front of the *shâla* or hall was made quite open, except the spaces between the walls and the first pillars from each end. In the sculptures at least of the second and third caves Vishṇu occupies the most prominent place, but the shrines of all three contain, or have once contained, the *linga* of Śiva: this, however, is probably a later substitution in the third cave, and in the second there is only a *chavaranga* or altar-pedestal for the *linga*. In style they vary much in details, but can scarcely differ much in age; and as the third contains an inscription of Mangaliśvara dated Śaka 500, *i.e.*, A.D. 578, we cannot be far wrong in attributing them all to the sixth century. The importance of this date can scarcely be over-estimated, as it is the first of the kind yet discovered in a Brahmanical cave. The inscription is by no means easily legible, and it occupied a good deal of my time to get a fair copy of it, and some letters quite defied my efforts to trace. Prof. Eggeling has been kind enough to look over and revise the proof of it, and to translate it.* When the other inscriptions I have

* See page 23.

brought home have also been translated, it is to be hoped some further information may be obtained throwing light both on the history of the architecture and of the people of the Kânaḍâ districts. I can only regret that my time and the means at my command did not admit of my copying many more inscriptions than I did.

Cave I. (photograph, Plate XVII.) is on the north-west of the hill, not more than a stone's throw from the nearest houses of the town, and only about fifty feet above the level of the houses. It is entered by a few steps, rising from what may have been a small court, but the decay of the rock has carried it away. Along the front, on each side of the steps, are the *gaṇa* of Śiva—dwarfs with human and bovine heads, capering and posing in all sorts of attitudes. Above the return of this base on the right or south-west side is a figure of Śiva 5 feet high, with the unusual number of eighteen arms dancing the Tâṇḍava;* Nandi, Gaṇapati, and the drummer being the only audience. The round earring in the right, and the elongated one in the left ear almost suggest that the sculptor had before him the head of an Arddhanâri. Between this figure and the cave is a small chapel with two pillars in its front standing on a base or raised step, the face of which is sculptured with rollicking *gaṇa*; and, as at Elephanta and on the four-armed figures that support the brackets in some of the Ajaṇṭâ caves, one of these *gaṇa* has a tortoise as a pendant to his necklace. Inside this chapel, round the ends and back, is a base covered with similar figures, two wrestling, one with a huge nose and a grinning face on his stomach, and another with a horse's head holding up a cobra. Above, on the back wall, is a pretty perfect figure of Maheśâsurî or Pârvatî as the destroyer of the buffalo demon Maheśa, 4 feet 7 inches high, four armed, holding up the buffalo like a pig by the tail, while the spear head—half the size of the buffalo's—is through the neck (Plate XIX. fig. 1). She holds the discus or *chakra* in one of her right hands, and the *shankh* or conch in the corresponding left. In the air above each shoulder is a pair of floating figures—male and female—the males holding some offering. On the right wall is Gaṇapati (Plate XIX. fig. 2), 3 feet 4 inches high, and on the left Skanda or Kârttikeya on his peacock, 2 feet 11 inches high.

At the left end of the front of the cave is a dwârapâla, 6 feet 2 inches high, with a thick cloth knotted outside his right thigh, and a triśula in his right hand. Below him is a figure composed of a bull and elephant in such a way that when the body of the bull is hid the elephant is distinctly seen, and when the body of the elephant is covered the remainder is a bull. Above the dwârapâla are Śiva and Pârvatî seated on a procumbent bull. (See Plate XX. fig. 2.)

The front of the veranda is supported by four pillars and two pilasters—two of the former broken through. The pillars are square, standing on a plain base, the first 4 feet of the shaft perfectly plain, then a square facia of elaborate carving, above this is an annulus of sixteen sides, then a thick plinth with arabesques supporting the bracket, the centre of which is filled with devices after the manner of Ajaṇṭa, the wings being filled with figures of Makaras, &c. Many of these devices both in this and the other caves are well deserving of being moulded. Over the brackets, against the architrave and hid from outside by the drip in front are a series of squat figures, all males, and each differing from his fellow, all two armed, supporting as it were, the roof above.

---

* For explanation of this see my *Elephanta*, § 69, and notes.

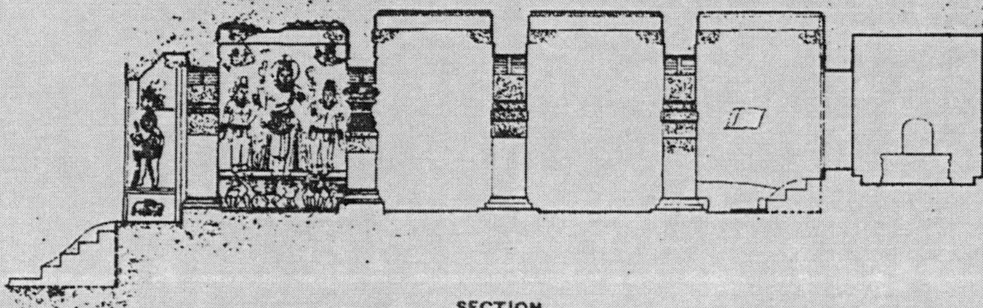

SECTION.

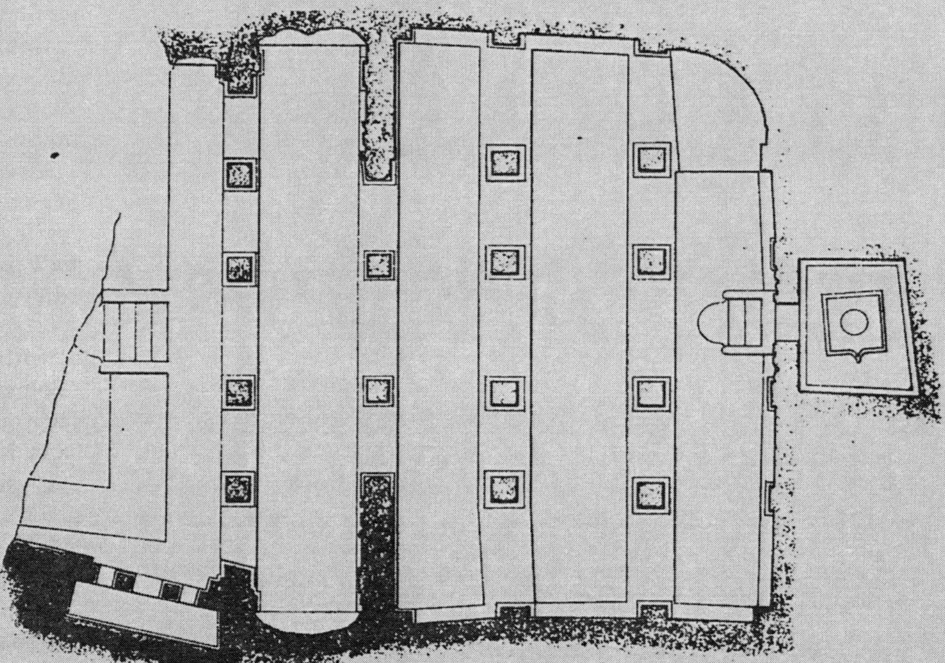

PLAN.

J. Burgess delt.

BADÂMI - CAVE I. DETAILS. PLATE XIX.

1

2

3

4

BADÂMI-CAVE I. DETAILS.

PLATE XX.

1. AT A.B. ON THE PLAN.

2

3

4

5

Inside the verandah at the left end, are three large figures: in the centre Śiva or perhaps more accurately, Harihara—the united form of Siva and Vishṇu, 7 feet 9 inches high, four armed, with skull and crescent on his *mugut*; a snake twists over the battle-axe in his upraised right hand; and he holds up a conch in his left (Plate XIX. fig. 4). The other two figures are females dressed in a sort of petticoat; that on his right is 6 feet high, with two *round* earrings, her right hand probably held a flower, but it is broken away. The other is 6 feet 3 inches high with a round earring in the right ear; the left ear is very much elongated and a round knob hangs by it; she holds up a flower in her left hand. Both the females (are they Satî and Pârvatî or Lakshmî and Pârvatî?) and Śiva have elaborate girdles and headgear, and the former have the heavy bracelets of many rings still worn by the wandering Vanjâris, Lambâdis, &c. Over each is the usual pair of floating figures—celestial attendants or whatever they may be—which are so frequent at Ajaṇṭâ and in all Bauddha caves, Below, between Śiva and the female, on his right is a bull-headed man (Nârada?) with a sceptre or long staff, and on the other side of Śiva is a dwarf or Pisâcha.

At the right end of the verandah is Arddhanâri, the united form of Śiva and Umâ or Pârvatî,* 7 feet 7 inches high, the female side with numerous rings on the ancles and forearm; she holds up a flower: the male side bears the axe and snake. Behind him is Nandi and Bringi, the latter 6 feet 2 inches high. On Umâ's left is a female 5 feet 9 inches high, in long petticoat and round head-dress, holding a box on her left shoulder. Over each side of the central figure is a pair of floating or flying figures. (Plate XIX. 3.)

The roof is divided by imitation beams into five compartments. In the middle one, within a circle of arabesques, 4 feet 7½ inches in diameter, is a figure of Śesha (Plate XX. 4—represented also on the cover of Mr. Fergusson's *Tree and Serpent Worship*). The central part or head and body are well formed and project boldly from the coil, but the left arm has been recently broken off. In the compartment to the right of this, on a boss or cloud, 2 feet 6½ inches in diameter, are a male and female, well cut, the male with a sword, and the female drawing forward a veil which floats out from behind her head and shoulders (fig. 5). In the corresponding compartment to the left are two rather smaller figures, not quite so well cut, the female with a sort of nimbus behind the head, and both holding flowers in their hands. In the end compartments are lotuses.

The dividing joists are supported by brackets carved in the form of men or animals—

all differing, and each issuing from a *makara's* head. Over the architraves above the front pillars is a moulding with dentils and leaves that strikingly resembles Greek patterns. Over this are groups of human figures, &c., and then another leaf moulding.

The entrance to the cave itself is three fifths of its whole width, or nearly 21 feet, divided by two pillars, with two half pillars at the sides (Plate XX. fig. 1). The pillars have simple bases, square shafts, the upper part of each ornamented with arabesques and birds, the capitals circular and somewhat in the style of the columns at Elephanta. The brackets are small but similar to those of the verandah. The half columns have the lower part of the shafts circular and fluted.

* On Arddhanâri or Arddhanârîśvara, see my *Elephanta*, § 38, and notes 57, 58. Such a figure is mentioned by Porphyry in the third century as being found in a cave in India. *Stobæus*, Lib. I. cap. iv. § 56, in ed. Heeren, Vol. I. pp. 140–142.

Inside, the cave measures 42 feet 1 inch wide, by about 24½ feet deep. It is not perfectly rectangular, and the south corner is a quadrant (see plan, Plate XVIII). The roof is supported by two rows of four columns each, parallel to the front, and similar to those of the verandah but somewhat higher. It is divided by joists and rafters into compartments: in the first, in front of the middle entrance, on a boss 3 feet 1 inch in diameter, are a pair of figures, the male with a sword and shield. (Plate XX. 3.) In the next, or central compartment, is a lotus answering to one on the floor. The others are plain.

The entrance to the shrine is poorly executed; it is approached by a few steps, and inside is the usual square *chavaranga* or altar, 4 feet 5 inches long and 4 feet 1 inch broad, with the spout to the south-west, and a small *linga* in the centre of it, 2 feet 2 inches high. The shrine is 8 feet 10 inches high, averages 9 feet 6 inches wide, and varies from 6 feet 11 inches to 8 feet 3½ inches deep. The drawings (Plates XVIII.-XX.) will illustrate this cave as far as it was possible to do so in the time, but it contains much sculpture deserving of careful delineation or even moulding. It is too dark for photography, and with only one School of Art student, and he a very slow operator, it was impossible to make more drawings in the time.

Cave II. (Plate XXI.) is considerably higher up the rock, to the east of Cave I., and faces north. In front of it are three lofty pinnacles of perpendicular rock. The front is raised a little above the level of the area before it, and the face of the basement is sculptured with gaṇa. Three steps have been built against the middle. At the ends of a platform or basement in front, 3 ft. 9 in. wide, are two dwârapâlas, 5 feet 10 inches high, each with a small female attendant. The verandah has four columns in front, 1 ft. 7½ in. square, and 8 ft. 10 in. high, very carefully and minutely carved from the middle upwards. Above them slender dragon brackets, in entire relief, project to support the drip, which is ribbed on the underside in imitation of wood. The central areas of the bracket capitals of the columns are filled with groups of imagery.

At the left or east end of the verandah is Varâha, the boar-headed incarnation of Vishṇu, with Śesha and Śeshinî below, and flying figures in the upper corners. (Plate XXIII. 2.) In a horse-shoe above is Vishṇu on Garuḍa, with attendants; and out of the *makara*-headed bracket issue two or three flying figures. At the west end of the verandah is a figure of Virâṭrûpa (fig. 1.)—the demiurge or creative manifestation of Vishṇu,—5 feet 1 inch high, with four arms, and his foot raised in combat with an enemy. This is a favourite representation on these caves, and in the older temples. On the base below are *gaṇa*. In a horse-shoe shaped compartment above is a ten-armed figure. On the compartment of the ceiling, just in front of this, is Vishṇu with four arms (Chatturbhûj) riding on Garuḍa, or Nâgântika, the half-man half-eagle *vâhana* or vehicle of Vishṇu;* and along the top of the wall, on a frieze, he is represented asleep on Śesha with many figures at his feet. On the next compartment of the ceiling is a fret with two figures in each corner. In the central square is a lotus and sixteen fishes round it; round them is a circle, circumscribed by a square, held by twelve small figures inside an outer square. The next compartment is a

* Conf. my *Elephanta*, § 39; Moore's *Hindu Pantheon*, pp. 98, 278, 288, 334, 335; Ward's *Hindus*, Vol. I. p. 256; H. H. Wilson's *Vishṇu Purâṇa* (1st ed.) p. 149, or 8vo. ed. Vol. II. p. 73; *Asiat. Res.*, Vol. VI. pp. 513, 514; Langlois's *Harivanśa*, tom. II. p. 79.

BADÂMI-FRONT OF CAVE II.

BADÂMI - PLAN OF CAVE II. PLATE XXII.

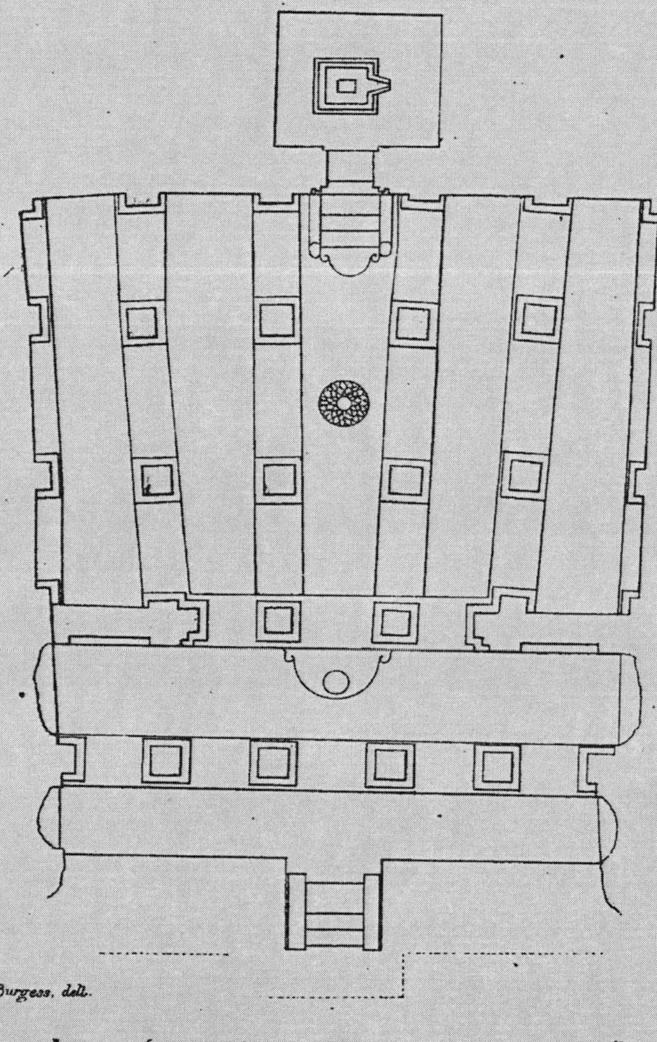

J. Burgess, delt.

Scale of 10 20 Feet

1.

From a photo.

2.

D. M.

BADÂMI - FRONT OF CAVE III FROM THE N. E.

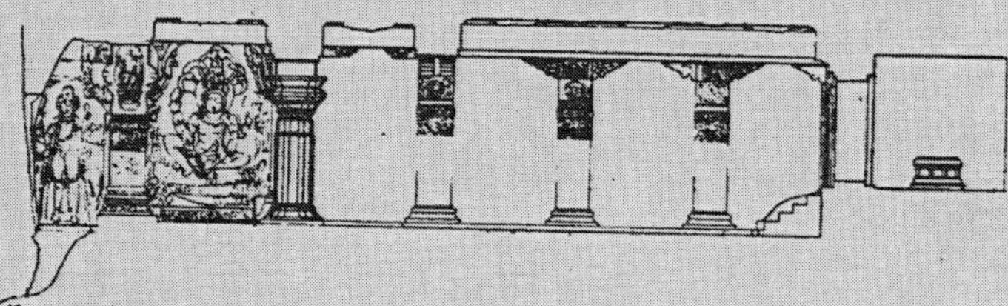

SECTION.

COLUMN. A.

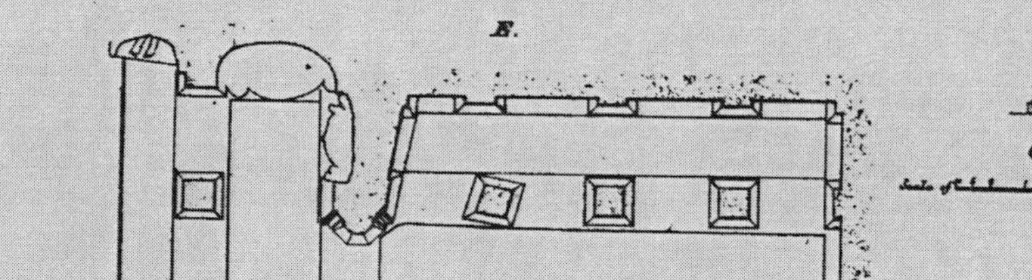

J. Burgess delt.

PLAN.

PLATE XXVI.

BADÂMI-CAVE III. EAST PILASTER OF THE VERANDA, &c.

fret with a lotus in the centre; and the last, at the east end, contains male and female flying figures.

The brackets supporting the beams across the verandah are strange vampire-like figures. The frieze of the cornice all round is carved with groups of numerous figures, representing Vishṇu asleep on Śesha, the churning of Sâgara by the Suras and Âsuras, &c.

The entrance from the verandah to the cave is similar to that in Cave I., with two pillars, 8 feet 6½ inches high, neatly carved with arabesques or figures in festoons, &c., standing on a step 7 inches above the level of the floor, and 3 feet wide.

Inside, the roof is supported by eight pillars, 9 feet 6½ inches high, standing on a low step 2 inches above the floor level, and arranged in four rows of two each from front to back, with pilasters corresponding against the walls. The *shâla* or hall measures 33 feet 4 inches wide, by 23 feet 7 inches deep, but is not quite rectangular, and 11 feet 4 inches high. (See plan, Plate XXII.) The brackets to the rafters are lions, human figures, vampires, elephants, &c. The shrine door is 2 feet 5 inches wide and 5 feet 11 inches high, and is ornamented above by the horse-shoe forms so common on Buddhist caves. It is approached by five steps which raise the floor of it 3 feet above that of the hall. The *chavaranga* or altar is square, but the linga that stood on it is gone. The cell measures 8 feet 9 inches by 7 feet 5½ inches. The verandah is 30 feet 4 inches by 6 feet 7 inches, and about 9 feet 11 inches high. The ceilings, except that of the verandah, are all plain, and the carving on the upper part of the pillars and the roof are thickly covered with smoke, from the cave having frequently been used to cook in. Some modern Vandal has broken the earrings and hands of the dwârapâla and the bow of Vishṇu in the verandah.

On the inside of the west pillar of the verandah is Lakshmî and the elephants, and on the inside of the pilaster is a fat figure squatting under a seven-headed snake; on others are love scenes, kissing, &c.

On the architrave, in the middle compartment, is a woman on a couch nursing a child, with two others behind and one at her head; then a man sitting; a head behind him; a woman standing with a child on her hip; then a child; a woman with a child in her arms; then five bullocks or cows; next a woman with a child at her foot, and a female head behind; then a woman pounding rice in a vessel towards which the last child stretches its hand; next a figure sitting with child on knee; and lastly a woman standing, In the scene on the opposite side of the verandah are men riding on lions, elephants, men, &c. To the west of the first-mentioned group, are four pairs, male and female, sitting in various positions. Opposite to this is a rather unintelligible composition. The east end compartment contains animals, and opposite it is a battle scene, to the west of which is the churning of the ocean by the Suras and Âsuras, already mentioned.

The figures in the brackets that support the cross-beams are well cut, some of them being very spirited.

The third cave is by far the finest of the series, and in some respects one of the most interesting Brahmanical works in India. Though it cannot compare with Elephanta or the Dumar Lena in size, it is still a large cave, the verandah measuring 70 feet in length, and the depth from front to the back wall being 48½ feet. It is considerably higher up the rock than Cave II., and is entered through a large square court in front of it, the north side of this court being formed by a large mass of rock, the east and west by walls of masonry. It is approached by a staircase through a door in the west side; and on the left of this door is a short inscription No. 12. The cave faces north, and the level of the floor is 8 or 9 feet above that of the court outside. The basement is built up in front with massive stones and is carved with *gaṇa*. (See photograph, Plate XXIV. and plan and section, Plate XXV.)

At the east end of the basement, outside the verandah, is Vishṇu as a dwârapâla, with eight arms (Ashṭabhuja), the left holding a bow, a shield, a conch, and the fourth resting against his haunch, the right hands hold sword, club, arrow, and discus. He wears a high ornamented *mugut* or cap, over which is a grinning bust, perhaps Nṛisiñha, holding the conch and *chakra* or discus. A sort of rope depends from Vishṇu's left ear and passes over his right shoulder. The dress is knotted behind the thighs. The eaves of the verandah project over this figure, and on the under side, just in front of his head, are six pairs of human figures in floating attitudes; two of the males are armed with sword and shield. On the face of the pilaster, at Vishṇu's left hand, is a sort of goat-headed bracket, similar to the figures over the door of Cave II. at Ajanṭâ. (See photograph, Plate XXVI.)

The verandah is supported in front by six square columns and two pilasters. Each pillar has three brackets, projecting one on each side, and one to the back or inside of the verandah. With one exception all the side brackets are carved with a male and female figure, in different attitudes on each; and each of the brackets, to the inside or roof of the verandah bears a tall female figure. The shoulders of the columns, as in the other caves, are carved with elaborate festoons, &c., and on each of the four sides of the lower portions of the shafts are medallions carved with groups of figures. A number, both of the brackets and medallions, have been drawn, but scarcely sufficiently well to do them justice. Photographs XXVI., XXIX., XXX. and XXXI., and of a portion of the sculpture under the drip or eaves in front of the central opening were taken, but the great heat, and accidents to chemicals, &c. prevented such extensive use of this means of illustration as might, under more favourable circumstances, have been attempted. Remains of painting are still distinctly traceable on the underside of the eaves, and on the carved roof of the verandah. Possibly traces might also be discovered on the larger images, but unfortunately they have been besmeared with whitewash by some photographer.

The full description of the sculpture on the front columns would occupy a good deal of space, but is almost unnecessary with the sketches that have been taken. Plates XXVII. and XXVIII. illustrate the brackets sufficiently:—

Plate XXVII. 1. is a sketch of the bracket on the face of the pilaster at the east end of the verandah: the same is shown from the other side in the photograph, Plate XXVI. The figures in it are among the best proportioned in the cave.

Fig. 2 represents the bracket facing the last on the left side of first pillar from the east end of the verandah. It is, perhaps, intended for Vishṇu with a five-hooded Ananta as a canopy over his head; but as the female has a single-hooded snake over her head, the tail of which the male figure holds in his right hand, it is possibly intended as a Nâga Râja and his consort. Her dress, as seems to have been the fashion with the Nâgas, is rather scanty below the hips.

Fig. 3 is the bracket on the west face of the same pillar, and represents a female fainting in the arms of a male figure. The loss of muscular power is well indicated by the doubling of her right ankle, the falling in of the left knee, the bending of the waist,

PLATE XXVII.

BADÂMI - SCULPTURED BRACKETS FROM THE VERANDA OF CAVE III.

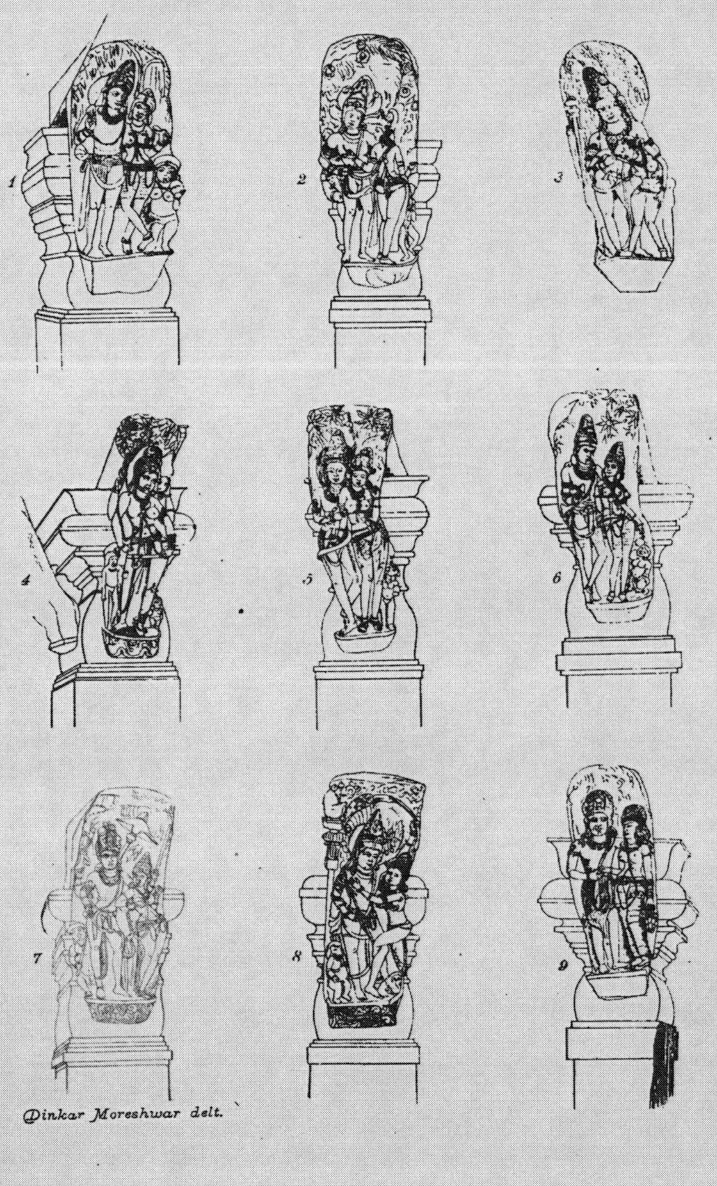

Dinkar Moreshwar delt.

BADÂMI-CAVE III. SCULPTURES. PLATE XXVIII.

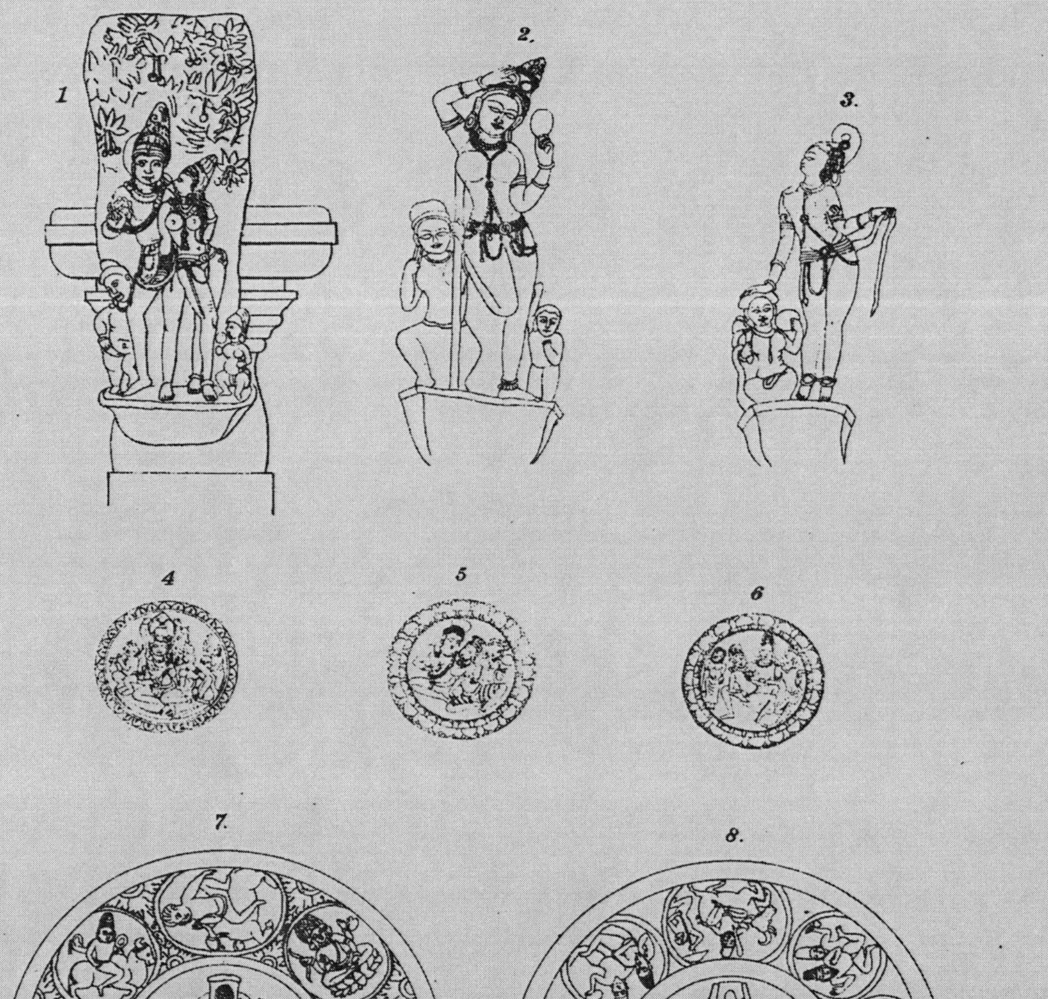

PLATE XXIX.

BADÂMI-VERANDA OF CAVE III FROM THE E. END.

BADÂMI-VERANDA OF CAVE III FROM THE W. END.

and the hanging of the hands. Her dress, like that on the last, consists principally of bracelets, necklaces, earrings, girdles, and the high cap.

Fig. 4 represents the bracket on the east side of the second column. It is a figure of Arddhanârîśvara—four armed, the right side male, the left female. In his upper right hand he holds up an axe or halbert, round which a cobra coils, and another hangs from the girdle round his loins. On his side of the high cap is a skull and crescent moon—Śiva's special emblems; and a Piśâcha or demon attends at his side. The female half, representing Parvâtî, holds up a mirror in the upper hand, and on the wrist, arm, and ankle, are the many ringed ornaments still affected by Vanjâris and aboriginal tribes. She is attended by her dwarf maid, carrying what may be, perhaps, her toilet requisites.*

Fig. 5 is the bracket on the west side of the same column, also representing a pair of figures with an attendant dwarf; the female, as in all these brackets, is on the left side of the male; and the part of the bracket over their heads is carved to represent foliage.

Fig. 6 is the corresponding one on the east side of the third pillar.

Figs. 7 and 8 represent the brackets on the west and east sides respectively of the fourth column of the verandah. On the former, the male figure is four armed, with a snake coiling round the shaft of his *paraśu* or battle-axe, another round his arm, and a third hanging from his loose girdle. He has the crescent of Śiva also on his high *mugut*, and the Piśâcha holds up an umbrella over his head. In the other the female is clinging to the male, who has a sceptre in his right hand, and the attendant dwarf is a Kinnara or horse-headed chorister.

Fig. 9 is the bracket on the east face of the sixth or west pillar. The head-dresses of the pair here represented, differ somewhat from the previous ones, and the female has a long skirt of striped cloth hanging to her ankles, the pattern of which is carefully wrought out in the stone.

Plate XXVIII. 1. represents the bracket on the west face of the third column. The bracket on the front of the pilaster at the west end of the verandah also is shown in the photograph, Plate XXXI.

Fig. 2 is the bracket on the inner side of the first column. Each of these brackets, projecting into the verandah, as has been already stated, consists of a single tall female with an attendant dwarf, standing under foliage.

Fig. 3 represents the corresponding one on the third column.

Specimens of the medallions on the lower part of the pillars may be seen in the photographs, Plates XXVI. and XXXI. Plate XXVIII., fig. 4, represents that on the east face of the first column, in which Nâga figures make their appearance. Figs. 5 and 6 are those on the east and west faces respectively of the fourth pillar.

At the west end of the verandah is a fine bold statue of Nṛisiñha or the lion-headed incarnation of Vishṇu, 11 feet high; at his right hand is a curly-headed Piśâcha, 3 feet 6 inches high, with thick lips and a tortoise as a brooch—the fellow of several at Elephanta. To the left of Nṛisiñha is a figure 4 feet 9 inches in height, with high turban, necklace, and jewelled belt and girdle. (See photograph Plate, XXIX.)

Beside this figure, on the back wall, is an equally tall figure of Śiva or Harihara.

* See my *Elephanta*, § 46.

At the east end is a colossal figure of Vishṇu sitting on the great snake Ananta (Plate XXX.), and in the back wall, beside this, is a gigantic figure of Varâha with Prithvî on his hand and Śesha below

Outside the verandah, at the west end, and on the return outwards of the rock, is a gigantic figure of Vishṇu, or Virâṭrûpa, the "all conquering-form," * similar to that in Cave II., but much larger, in active conflict with his enemy. (See Plate XXXI.)

The roof of the verandah is divided into compartments, each filled with numerous sculptures, as are also the fronts of the architraves or friezes over the columns in front of the great hall. Plate XXVIII. 7, is a rough sketch of the sculpture in the central compartment of the roof, and fig. 8 is the compartment next to the west of it. The verandah is separated from the central hall by four columns and pilasters. (See Drawings and Ground Plan, Plate XXV.

Within these columns is the front aisle of the cave, the roof of which is again divided into compartments, in the central one are a male and a female figure among clouds, the male with a sword and small shield. In the compartments, right and left of this, are lotuses.

The roof of the hall is divided into nine compartments, by divisions very slightly raised from the level of the ceiling. In the central one of the front row is a man riding on a ram, with other figures, one before and another behind. In the compartment to the right or west of this is a pair of flying figures, the male with a sword, but the group is defaced. In the left is a male with a sword, holding a shield overhead, and with him a small female. In the next row we have, in the centre, Brahma on a swan, which apparently pecks at a figure which touches Brahma's hand with his. In one of his left hands Brahma holds what appears to be a bag, and in the other a *málá* or rosary, and a male touches his cheek with his hand. In the compartment to the right of this again is a *deva* on a *makara*, holding up a circle or large ring. In the corresponding one on the left are three figures on an elephant, the second holding an umbrella over the first (Indra ?). In the back row—in the centre is a *deva*, three-faced, like Brahma, on a swan, and holding a *triśula* in his right hand, his left resting on his knee. Chauṅri bearers accompany him before and behind. In the square to the left or east are two flying figures, the male with an offering and the female with a round fan or mirror; in that to the right are a pair of flying figures, the male with a sword; but the group is damaged. The roofs of the side aisles are plain.

A rubble wall has been built in modern times across from the third pillar on the inner side of the verandah to the back of the cave; and the floor of the verandah has been dug out in holes in a way that it is difficult to conjecture the object of it.

The full delineation of these Badâmi caves might be executed without much trouble by a few School of Art students under proper direction, and, if well done, would form a valuable illustration of Vaishṇava mythology and Indian art, only to be equalled by what Ajaṇṭâ affords for Buddhism.

Until the discovery and translation of the inscription (No. 7, Plate XXXII.) in this cave, on a pilaster, beside the figure of Vârâha, no suspicion of their antiquity was entertained. Major Biggs had photographed it to a scale of about one-fifteenth of the original, but it was so small and indistinct that "not a single line could be deciphered

* See Moor's *Hindu Pantheon*, pp. 179, 327.

PLATE XXXI.

BADAMI-VIRATARUPA AT THE W. END OF CAVE III.

7. BADÂMI-INSCRIPTION IN CAVE III :-DATED ŚAKA 500.-A.D. 578.

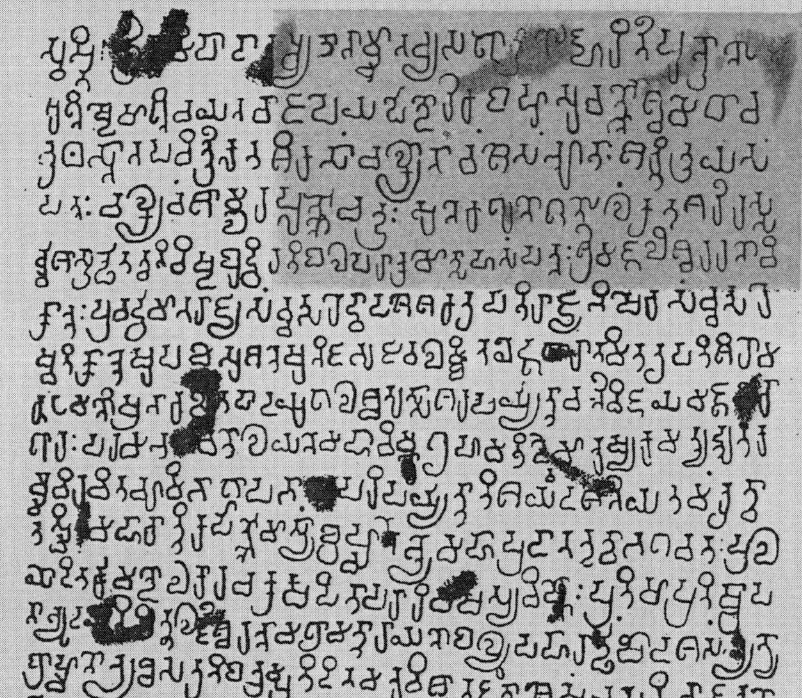

J. Burgess, fecit.

43 by 25 inches.

8

Size, 2 ft. 2 in. by 1 ft. 9 in.

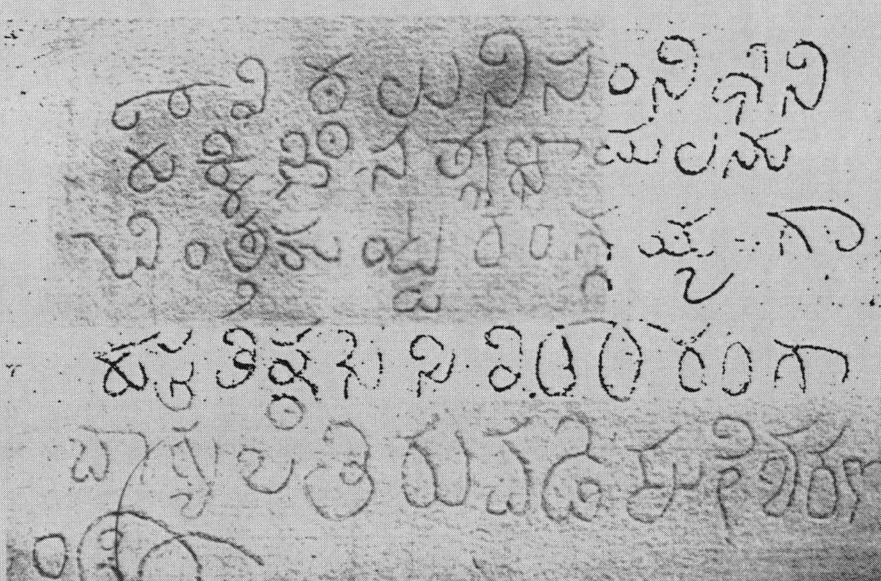

9

Size, 2 ft. 2 in. by 1 ft. 6 in.

with confidence," nor the date or the king's name made out.* There are three other inscriptions on columns in the same cave, of which I obtained excellent "estampages" (Nos. 8, 9, Plate XXXIII., and 10, Plate XXXIV.), and one of these contains the figures of the date Saka 1426, or A.D. 1514. The inscription is clearly cut in Kanarese, and Professor Eggeling reads the commencement of it, *Sâḷivâhana śaka varshambulu* 1426 *gunaḍ*(h)*i pramâthisaṁvatsara Âshâḍhaba* 11. Yet Dr. Bird, the only antiquary who had previously examined the caves, says † the date in this inscription "is called *Nákula hâla nawakâla mritana ghaya* 1476, नाकुहाल नवकाल मृतनगय १४७६, or the new date of *Hala Hala*, the name for Buddha, or a Jaina saint. The date is probably intended for a new adaptation of the era of *Buddha* Śakya, B.C. 543, and, if so, would give the date of these caves, A.D. 933." This may show how little we can depend on either his readings or translations; still this, and some further equally crude conjectures, was sufficient to convince this amateur that these caves belonged to the tenth century, though the characters of an inscription in it are of the sixth. The inscription (Plate XXXII.) measures about 43½ inches in height, and consists of twenty-four lines, each about 25 inches in length. It was copied with great difficulty, the stone being worn, and the letters, never deeply cut, being in some places almost illegible. Two or three "estampages" were taken, and a careful tracing made from them, using the best portions of each; this was then compared in all the less distinct places with the stone. It has been submitted to Professor Eggeling, who has kindly favoured me with the following transliteration and translation :—

Transliteration.

Svasti ‖ Śrîsvâmipâdânudhyâtânâm Mânavyasagotrâṇâṁ Hârîtiputrâṇâm agnishṭomâgnichayanavâjapeyapauṇḍarîkabahusuvarṇṇâśvamedhâvabhṛithasnânapavitrîkṛitaśirasâṁ Chalkyânâṁ vaṁśe sambhûtaḥ śaktitrayasaṁpannaḥ Chalkyavaṁśâmbarapûrṇṇachandraḥ anekaguṇagaṇâlaṅkṛitaśarîras sarvvaśâstrârtthatatvanivishṭabuddhir atibalaparâkramotsâhasaṁpannaḥ śrî Maṅgalîśvaro raṇavikrântaḥ pravarddhamânarâjyasaṁvvatsare dvâdaśe Śakanṛipatirâjyâbhishekasaṁvvatsareshv atikrânteshu pañchasu śateshu nijabhujâvalambitakhaḍgadhârânamitanṛipatiśiromakuṭamaṇiprabhârañjitapâdayugalaś chatussâgaraparyantâvanivijayamangali(*lai?*)kâgâraḥ paramabhagavato layane mahâvishṇugṛiham. atidaivamânushyakam atyadbhutakarmmavirachita(*ṁ*) bhûmibhâgopabhâgopariparyantâtiśayadarśanîyatamam kṛitvâ tasmin mahâkârttikapaurṇṇamâsyâṁ brâhmaṇebhyo mahâpradânan datvâ bhagavataḥ pralayoditârkkamaṇḍalâkârachakrakshapitâpakâripakshasya Vishṇoḥ pratimâpratishṭhâpanâbhyudaye *Nipinma*(?)lingeśvaran ‡ nâma grâman nârâyaṇabalyupahârârthaṁ shoḍaśasaṁykhebhyo brâhmaṇebhyaś cha satranibandham pratidinam anuvidhânan kṛitvâ śeshaṁ cha parivrâjakabhojyan dattavân sakalajaganmaṇḍalavanasamarthâya rathahastyaśvapadâtasaṁkulânekayuddhalabdhajayapatâkâvalambita chatussamudrormmivâritayaśaḥpratânopaśobhitâya devadvijagurupûjitâya jyeshṭhâyâsmadbhrâtre Kîrttivarmmaṇe parâkrameśvarâya tatpuṇyopachayaphalam âdityâgnimahâjanasamaksham udakapûrvvaṁ viśrâṇitam asmadbhrâtṛiśuśrû(*sha*)ṇe yat phalam tan mahyaṁ syâd iti na kaiśchi(*t*) parihâpayitavyaḥ ‖ bahubhir vvasudhâ dattâ bahubhiś chânupâlitâ | yasya yasya yadâ bhûmiḥ tasya tasya tadâ phalam ‖ svadattâṁ paradattâṁ vâ yatnâd raksha Yudhishṭhira | mahîr mmahîkshitâṁ śreshṭhaṁ dânâch chhreyo 'nupâlanam ‖ svadattâṁ paradattâṁ vâ yo hareta vasundharâm | śvavishṭhâyâṁ kṛimir bhûtvâ pitṛibhis saha majjati ‖ Vyâsagîtâḥ ślokâḥ ‖

---

* *Inscriptions in Dharwar and Mysore,* No. XII., and *Jour Bomb. B.R. Asiat. Soc.* Vol. IX. p. 318.

† *Historical Researches on the origin and principles of the Bauddha and Jaina Religions* (Bombay 1847), pp. 50, 51.

‡ The inscription is abraided here, and traces of letters might also be doubtfully read *Tipitma.*

Translation.

May it be well! in the race of the Chalkyas [for *Châlukyas*], worshippers of the feet of the lord (*Vishṇu*), members of the Mânavyagotra, sons of Hârîti, whose heads are purified with sacred ablutions after the performance of the Agnishṭoma, Agnichayana, Vâjapeya, Pauṇḍarîka, Bahusuvarṇa, and Aśvamedha rites—was born one who being endowed with the three (*regal*) powers and possessed of extraordinary strength, bravery, and perseverance, is the full moon in the firmament of the Chalkya race, his person being adorned with a numberless series of virtues, whilst his mind is embued with the essence of the objects of all sciences Śrî Mangalîśvara who—victorious in battle, in the twelfth year of (*his*?) reign, five hundred years having passed since the coronation of the king of the Śakas, (*A.D. 578*,)—having made his feet brilliant with the glitter of the jewels of the diadems of kings whose heads he bent by the edge of the sword wielded by his own arm, and having by the conquest of the earth bounded by the four oceans, become the (*sole*?) receptacle of prosperity,—after building on the site of the most holy (*Vishṇu*) a house of the great Vishṇu surpassing all things divine and human, constructed by most wonderful labour and highly conspicuous by means of enclosing boundaries on the chief and adjoining grounds *; and having in this (*temple*) on the great full moon of Kârttika made a grand gift to the Brahmans,—has, at a festival held for the inauguration of an image of the holy Vishṇu, who destroys the hosts of enemies with his *chakra* which has the shape of the orbit of the sun rising on the dissolution of the universe,—arranged for the revenues of the village named Nipinma-(or *Tipitma*-)lingeśvara (?) to be applied for daily making offerings to Nârâyaṇa and giving charitable relief to sixteen Brâhmans, distributing such food as remains to be eaten by mendicants.

This grant is made in the presence of the sun, the fire, and the people, after pouring out water, for the benefit and to increase the religious merit of my eldest brother Kîrttivarman, the lord of valour and beloved of gods, twice born and gurus, who was equal to rule the multitudinous countries of the entire earth; and was adorned with the creepers of fame depending down from the standards of victory gained in many battles thronged with chariots, elephants, horses, and footmen; and only checked by the waves of the four seas. By many earth is given, and by many it is preserved; whoever at any time is in possession of the ground, he at that time enjoys the fruit thereof. Guard thou diligently, O Yudhishṭhira, that (ground) which is given by thyself or by another; land is the most valuable gift of kings; and better than giving is protecting. He who takes away ground given by himself or by another, together with his ancestors, becomes a worm and is immersed in dog's ordure.—Verses composed by Vyâsa.

The fact that this inscription, in the characters used in the sixth century, is dated in A.D. 578, six years older than another from Aiwaḷḷi, read by the late Dr. Bhâu Dâjî, and that the oldest temples at Badâmi, Paṭṭadkal, and Aiwaḷḷi all bear one general architectural character and must therefore belong to one age, opens up a new province in the history of Indian architectural history; for hitherto we had scarcely any buildings with inscriptional dates between the fourth or fifth and the ninth or tenth centuries. These caves being now proved to be of the sixth, and possibly one of them of the fifth,

* Should we read: bhûmibhâgopabhogopari paryantâtiśayadarśanîyatamaṁkṛitvâ, and translate, "and having over and above the usufruct of a piece of ground, made it (*the temple*) highly conspicuous by means of enclosing boundaries," &c.?

BÂDÂMI-CAVE III. INSCRIPTIONS. PLATE XXXIV.

10

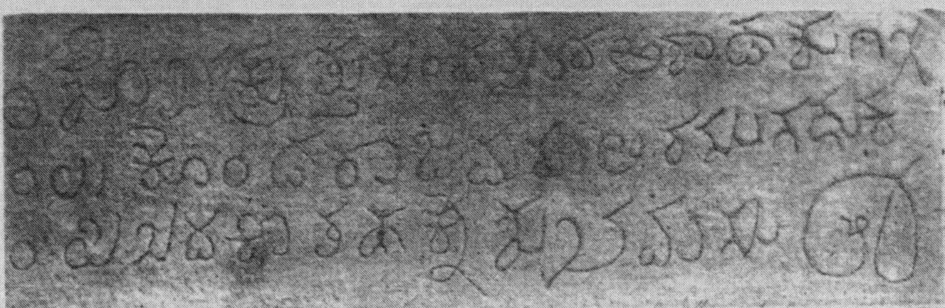

11

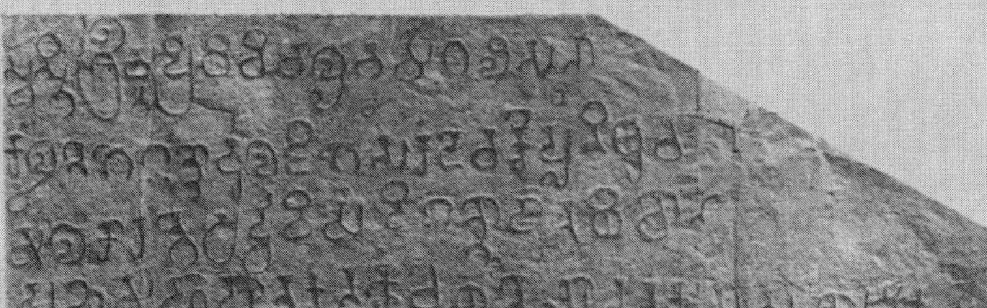

12.

13

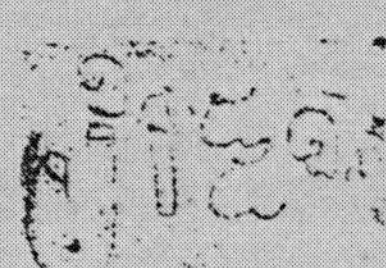

14.

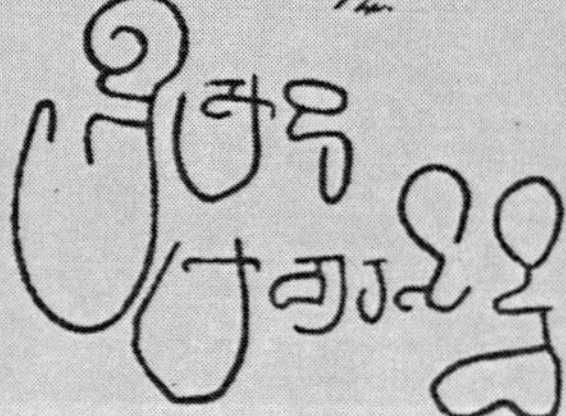

15.

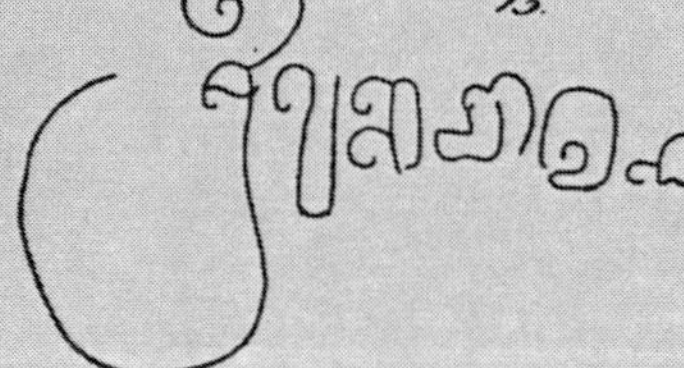

16.

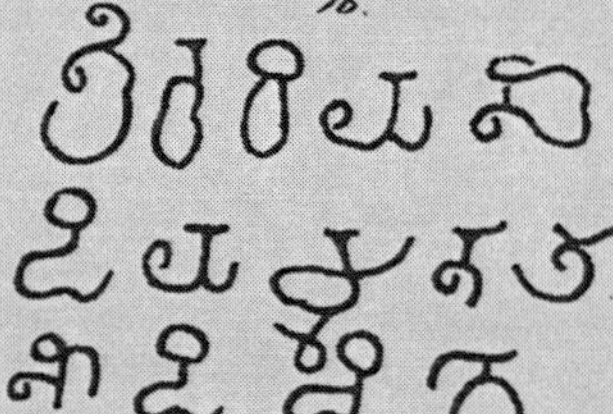

17.

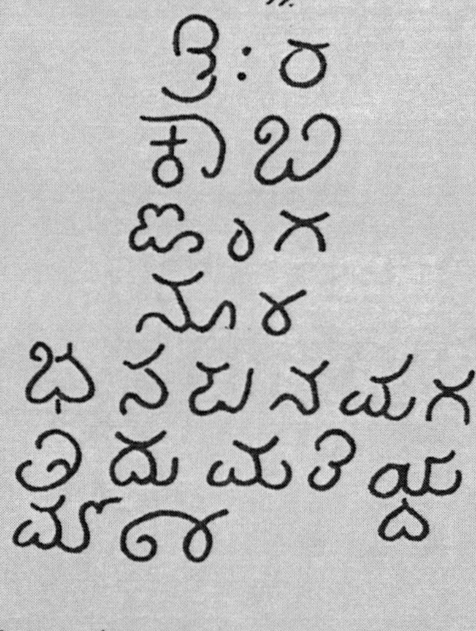

18.

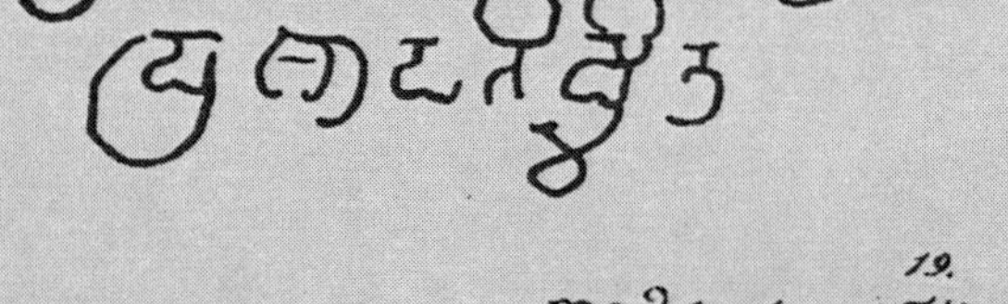

19.

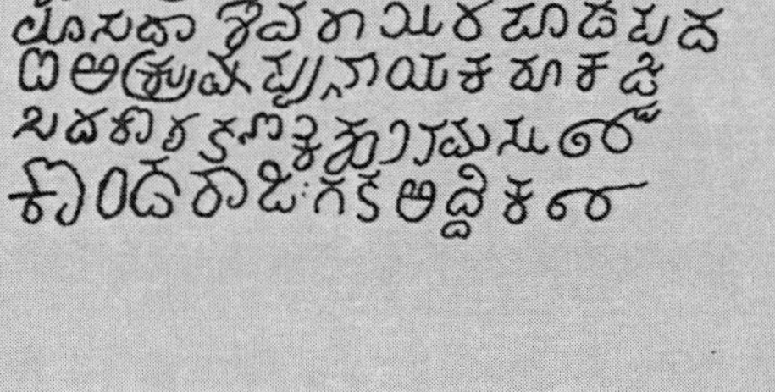

W. Griggs, Photo-lith.

BADÂMI - THE JAINA CAVE No. IV. PLATE XXXVI.

1. PLAN.

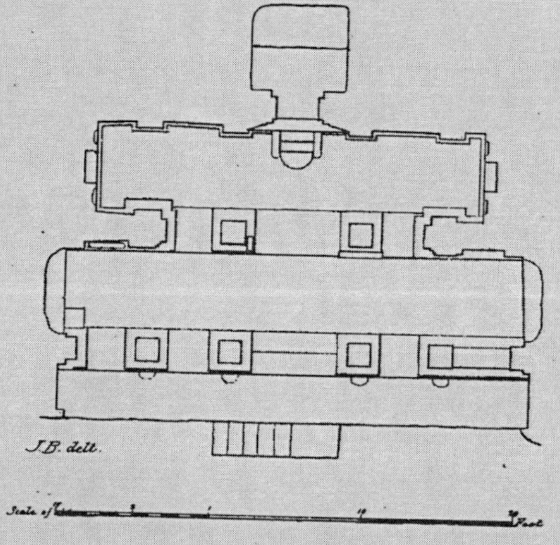

2.

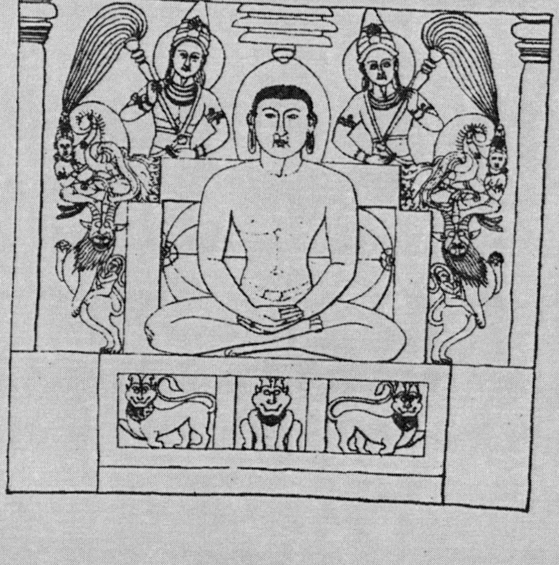

3.

PLATE XXXVII.

BADÂMI - VERANDA OF CAVE IV FROM THE W. END.

we shall be obliged to assign some of the many very old temples at Aiwaḷḷi also to the fifth, the fine temple known as the Durga to the seventh, and others to the eighth century. In fact within a stretch of fifteen miles we have the history of art in this district for at least seven centuries. But instead of six weeks to survey it, it would be well worth a three months' examination, with a couple or more of expert draughtsmen, a skilled paṇḍit, and the expense of a cartload of moulds.

On the rock to the left of the cave is an inscription (No. 11), and in different places some smaller ones, apparently names; see Nos. 13, 14, 15 (Plates XXXIV., XXXV.).

To the east of Cave III. is a great fissure in the rock; and a little beyond this, and on a slightly lower level than the last, is the Jaina Cave. It faces north by west and consists of a verandah with four pillars, an inner cave or antechamber with two pillars in front, and up five steps is the shrine. The scale of the cave is much smaller than that of the others: the verandah is only 31 feet in length by 6 feet 7 inches wide, and the whole depth of the cave is about 16 feet. The shrine measures 6 feet 4 inches by 5 feet 10 inches (see plan, Plate XXXVI.). The details, however, allowing for difference of mythology, are much the same as in the other caves, and it may be attributed to about the same age. There are medallions filled with flower patterns on the lower parts of the shafts of the pillars of the verandah, and on the brackets are horned *siñhas*—one knocked off. On the inside of the eaves is a fat figure with a hand on each knee. At the west end of the verandah is Parśvanâtha, 7 feet 4½ inches high, with a five-hooded snake over him as a sort of nimbus. A female on the right side with a nâga hood holds up the rod of the umbrella which shades him. There is a fat lugubrious-like figure below, with necklace and *janvi*—or Brahmanical thread; above is another unfinished. Outside the verandah, at this end, is a small image of a tîrthañkara and a worshipper. At the end of the antechamber is a compartment divided into three: above is a Jina 2 feet 8 inches high, and on each side of him four rows of three Jinas, each 6½ inches high; below this; in a division 2 feet 8 inches by 1 foot 7 inches, are four Jinas, each 1 foot 4 inches high, all standing, with fans at each side of each head; the lowest division, 2 feet 8 inches by 7 inches, contains five sitting Jinas, each with fans. There is also a standing figure of a Jina outside the compartment to the right. The pillars that separate the verandah from the inner apartment are also carved with numerous small figures of Jinas. See Plate XXXVII.

At the east end of the verandah is a standing Jina, 7 feet 8 inches high, with two snakes coiling round his legs, their heads rising from his feet towards his hands. He has elongated ears, and two ringlets of hair fall down upon his shoulders. On the right and left kneeling females worship him (photograph, Plate XXXVII.) The nudity of all the figures shows that the cave belonged to the Digambara Jainas.

On the centre of the roof are two flying figures and a fragment of painting. All the brackets are human busts in the mouths of *makaras*.

In the west end of the antechamber is a standing Jina 6 feet 5 inches high, with a canopy of flowers over the head. At the back near this, among many other purely Jaina figures, is one, apparently of Lakshmî, with a bird as a *chinha* or cognizance over her high *mugut:* she is four-armed and sits under a tree. There is also a four-armed male figure with an elephant as his *chinha*. On the back wall is Parśvanâtha with the seven-headed cobra coiled from side to side behind him (Plate XXXVI. 3). Over him is an umbrella or canopy.

At the east end is another **Jina**, 6 feet 8 inches high, with curly hair and ringlets falling over the shoulders, and low down are the same two devatas as at the other end under trees—**Lakshmî** and a male figure with high caps. The door of the shrine is sculptured with flowers, and has a dwârapâla 2 feet 7 inches high on each side; over the lintel are horse-shoe ornaments with flowers within, and at the ends sitting Jinas. In the shrine is a *siñhasana* or lion-throne, 2 feet 3½ inches high, with a central and two side lions in front. On it is a sitting **Tîrthañkara** 4 feet 7 inches high and 2 feet 8 inches across the shoulders, naked, with nimbus behind the head, and a cushion behind the back. The back of the seat is represented in the usual way, with makara heads at the ends of the cross-bar, &c. Over the nimbus is a triple *chatra*, and behind it a tree. A chauṅri-bearer behind each shoulder wears a high cap, and above are two flying figures. The sculpture has been but roughly finished. (Plate XXXVI. 2.) There is a separate image of **Mahâvîra** lying in the verândâ.

On the rock, at the west side of this cave, are some small inscriptions of names; they were photographed on a small scale by Major Biggs, but two of them cannot be read on the photograph. Dr. Bhâu Dâjî transliterated them—" (1) Chivarika. (2) Śrî " Vimimmana. (3) Śrî Kuda Svâmi. (4) Śri Da . . . . . . *or* Va . . . . . . (5) Śrî " Dandadeva. (6) Śrî Gehpahana (Gehruana ?). (7) Śrî Akimi *or* Arimi. (8) Mâgâna. " (9) Śrî Prapannabuddhi *or* Prasannabudhi. (10) Śrî Kana." The alphabet he considered to be of the sixth century, and the names those of Jaina Sâdhus or holy men of the Digambara sect.*

The **Jina** in the fifth Cave, if cave it can be called, at the head of the lake, is a pretty well carved figure: he holds up his right hand with a small rosary, and with the forefinger and thumb touching. He wears a *jânvi* and several necklaces, anklets, bracelets, and a sort of epaulette.

A little to the north-west of this is a small shrine built against a rock, on which is carved **Vishṇu** reposing on **Śesha**, and not only **Brahma** springing from his navel, but a whole host of *devatas* arranged around on a sort of rainbow. There are also two pieces of mythological carving on the walls.

On the north-west side of this rock are a number of Vaishṇava carvings—**Varâha**, **Nṛisiñha**, **Maheśâsurî**, **Gaṇapati**, **Brahma**, &c., and below them sitting **Yogis** with snake canopies. There is a *linga* at the corner, and others in compartments on the west face of the rock.

North of this is a number of old shrines. One is a low maṇḍap and shrine with *pradakshina* or circumambulatory passage round it: in the shrine is a figure kneeling on a Yoni, resting his hand on the right knee which is up: the left arm is broken off. The four columns in the maṇḍap are similar to those at Belgâm with a very thin torus under the abacus. The temple faces south.

Eastwards is a very massive old temple—possibly of the eighth or ninth century. The four pillars of the inner maṇḍap are very heavy square blocks with scarcely any carving. On one of them is the inscription No. 16. Though the columns are short, the roof is considerably raised by the supporting lintels which are very deep. The roof slants down outside. The temple is Dravidian in style, and faces west. Over the doors of

* *Jour. Bomb. B.R. As. Soc.* Vol. IX. p. 317.

some small shrines on the same platform are Lakshmî and the elephants. On a pillar in a smaller temple to the east of it is the inscription No. 17, Plate XXXV.

West of this again is another old temple surrounded by a number of smaller shrines which are now occupied by some of the villagers for dwellings and cowhouses. It faces south, and has Lakshmî over the door. By the side of it are a heap of snake stones. I intended to have copied some of them, but did not find time for doing so; this, however, is to some extent compensated for by the specimens drawn from instances occurring elsewhere. (See p. 43 and Plate LVI.)

On a crag of the hill to the north-east of the Dharmaśâla is an old temple with massive square pillars, and having on the right side of the door the inscription No. 18.

The temple faces east by south, and on the left side of the door is a dwârapâla with sword and shield; above this are smaller figures of two women with children. The dwârapâla on the right side is defaced. The porch has four square pillars, and on one of them is the inscription No. 19. The door has simple mouldings round it. The door of the shrine has two pilasters a little in advance of it; a fat figure on the lintel, with females at the bottom of the jambs; and between the jamb and the pilaster is a recess in which is a dwârapâla with a club, holding a figure, half human female and half goat, by the hair.

Round the outside, above the base, is a band of well carved *gaṇa*, and over this is a course of horse-shoe ornaments, each with a human head inside. Above this again is a row of animals' heads—lions, elephants, griffons, &c.—some of them rather grotesque. In a compartment above, on the south side is an *alto rilievo* statue of Śiva, four-armed, with cobra and triśula, and two attendants, the one on the left with moustache. In a similar compartment on the north side is a four armed statue of Vishṇu (Chaturbhûja) with nimbus, *chakra* and *shankh*, and male and female attendants.

This temple has a linga in it, but is quite deserted, and is infested both by bats and wild beasts—panthers or leopards, Had time permitted I would have made a plan and endeavoured to obtain some sketches from it. It is evidently much older than the second inscription would indicate.

There are many inscriptions in Badâmi and the immediate neighbourhood that it seems very desirable to copy, but to do so satisfactorily demands much time and patient care.

A short distance south from Badâmi is Bânaśankari, a tîrtha or place of pilgrimage of some note in the neighbourhood. Here is a tank about 400 feet square, surrounded on all sides except the west by a colonnade or covered walk. On the west side is a maṇḍap supported by twenty-four columns—in four rows of six each—also a *dipdân*, or tower for lights, consisting of a basement eight or nine feet high, supporting three stories and the usual pillar or spire; the upper part at least is modern. At each end of this west side of the tank is a gateway into the court.

West from the first-mentioned building are fragments of four small towers, two of them in the court of the temple: they are probably old dipdâns. The present temple is a granite building of quite recent date, with a Muhammadan dome of small size and no proportion on the top of the *śikhar* or spire, which rises from a broken square and changes into a duodecagon. In the compound, lying on its back, is a slab with part of a Kanarese inscription, and on the base of a large column belonging to some older temple is a long one scarcely legible. The former, I believe, is No. XXII. of the volume of *Inscriptions in Dharwar, &c.*, published in 1866, but as I was unable to procure a copy of that work, I was deprived of its almost invaluable guidance, both here and elsewhere. This inscription "is dated," says Dr. Bhâu Dâjî, "Śâlivâhana Śâka 1423 (*i.e.* A.D. 1501), and is in Sanskrit and Kanarese. It commences with a Sanskṛit verse in praise of Śiva; the verse is to be found at the commencement of the *Harshacharita* of Bâṇa-bhaṭṭa, who wrote in the seventh century, and is evidently quoted in this inscription and others recording grants of land in this volume. The verse in praise of Gaṇapati is the composition of the learned commentator Mallinâtha, in his *Tîkâ* or (commentary) on the *Megha Dûta* or *Cloud Messenger* of Kalidâsa. The name of a king Achyuta Râya is found; he has the titles Sakala Sâmanta Chakra Mukuta Mani Marìchi Manjari Virâjita Charana Kamala Râjendra śekhara Śrîmat Mahârâjadhirâja Parameśvara Śrî Vîrapratâpa."*

To the north of the great temple is an old one of Draviḍian style; the roof of the manḍap or *naos* gone, and the whole structure half buried in the earth. There are also other fragments of buildings all round, but none of them appeared to be very old. Near the old half-buried temple is a fine tall pillar of eight sides below and sixteen above. Some obscene pieces of sculpture lie about.

Outside the north gate stands the wooden car of the idol, with stone wheels about eight feet in diameter.

To the east of Badâmi, among the hills, I visited Alai Tîrtha. A fair or *mela* is held there, and there are some small cells, probably old structures, and a number of sculptures, with an inscription carved on the rock.

PAṬṬADKAL.

In the end of March I reached Paṭṭadkal, the "Purudkul" of Major Biggs' photographs, on the Mâlaprabhâ, about nine miles east by south, in a straight line from Badâmi, and just opposite the village of Kâtâpur, where iron smelting is briskly carried on by a few natives. The number of old temples remaining here, and still more the number that must have been pulled down in very recent times, over an area extending considerably to the north of the village, are evidences that at one time, probably now very remote, Paṭṭadkal must have been a place of no small repute. And Aiwaḷḷi, at a short distance to the east of this, being also equally rich in remains of the sixth, seventh, and eight centuries of our era, might suggest that the famous Vatapipura, the capital of the Châlukya dynasty of the Kanara country was possibly in this neighbourhood. We learn, at least, from an inscription at the village of Amnibhavi, four or five miles from Dhârwâḍ, that in A.D. 567 Satyâśrâya, the son of Kirttivarma, was ruling or residing at Keśuvalala, on the banks of this same Mâlaprabhâ or Mâlapahârî river.

But of all the ancient temples at both these villages, only one, the great temple at Paṭṭadkal, is now in use for purposes of worship. At Paṭṭadkal the others still standing are occupied by people living near them as sheds for cattle, or by individuals to live in and blacken with the smoke of their cooking fires. Even the great temple wants

* *Jour. Bomb. B. R. As. Soc.* vol. ix. p. 321.

PLATE XXXVIII.

PAṬṬADKAL - GREAT SAIVA TEMPLE.

PAṬṬADKAL - THE GREAT SAIVA TEMPLE. PLATE XXXIX.

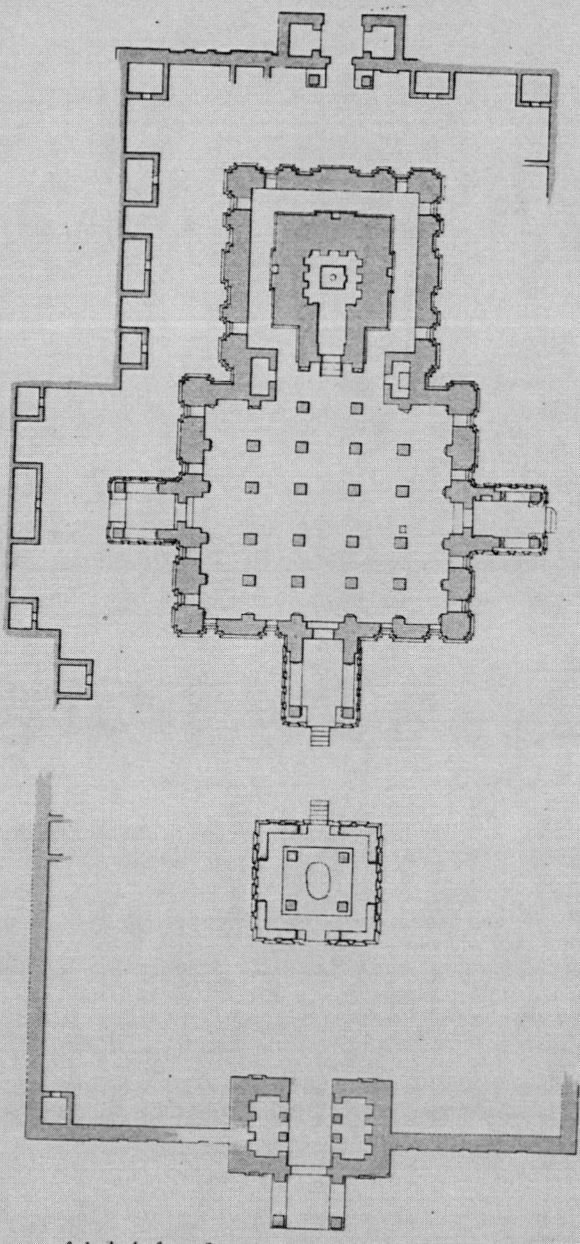

J. Burgess, delt.

some of the slabs from the roof, and must admit the rain very freely in the monsoon. But the villagers show a large field, once covered with temples, which they have carried entirely away (except, in several cases, the *lingas*—left from superstitious reasons), and over the foundations of which they raise their crops; and, unless some effort be made to stop the demolition, others on the same side of the village will follow.

In the village of Aiwaḷḷi, many of the temples have been converted into dwelling houses, stables, cowhouses, &c. On the outskirts, many are lying complete ruins, as if pulled down by the Wadâris or stonemasons for the sake of the fine blocks of stone forming the shafts of the pillars and lintels. A little farther from the village, dozens are standing, overgrown with jungle brushwood, and partially filled by earth and sand, only awaiting a visit from these worst enemies of ancient art, who, having no reverence for ought but money, for the sake of a few annas, will break up the finest sculpture or the most interesting inscription, if only the stone on which it is can be roughly squared for a lintel to a cowshed or a post for a gate. There was a large encampment of them at Aiwaḷḷi in April.

The larger temples at Paṭṭadkal are all pure examples of the Draviḍian or southern style of architecture. As described by Mr. Fergusson,* "they are all square pyramids, divided into distinct storeys, and each storey ornamented with cells, alternately oblong and square. Their style of ornamentation is also very much coarser than that of the Châlukya style, and differs very much in character. The domical termination of the spires is also different and much less graceful." These Draviḍian temples of an early age, he afterwards adds, "are wanting in all that elegance of form and detail which is so characteristic of the Châlukya style, but are not without a purpose-like boldness of form, expression of stability, and a certain amount of grandeur, though this is, of course, more easily observant in the larger examples in the south of India, than it is in those at Paṭṭadkal. If, on the other hand, we compare it with the more modern temples, it will be seen how much the form lost by the gradually growing steepness of outline and attenuation of details. The modern forms are not without a certain degree of elegance which is wanting in the more ancient; but in all the higher characteristics of design the older are by far the finest examples."

The great temple at Paṭṭadkal, with the canopy over the Nandi or sacred bull, in front of it, has been enclosed in a large quadrangle surrounded by little cells or shrines, much in the style of the Jaina temples. Huts now occupy the sites of some of these, others are used to store grain in, and more are destroyed. It had a massive gateway in front, and a small one behind; possibly, also, there were gates on the north and south sides, but this is quite uncertain. The floor of the temple is raised by five or six steps above the level of the court. The great hall is entered by three doorways, with porches in the east front, and on the north and south sides, and measures 50 feet 8 inches from north to south, by 45 feet 10 inches from east to west. The roof of this is supported by sixteen columns, disposed in four rows—massive blocks, each about 2 feet 5 inches square, without proper bases. At the west end of this hall are two more pillars, 8 feet 6 inches apart, and beyond them is the shrine, entered by a lobby, about a foot above the level of the floor. The shrine is 12 feet square, and is surrounded by a *pradakshina* or passage for circumambulation, at the entrance to which, on each side

* *Architecture in Dharwar and Mysore*, p. 63.

of the front of the shrine, is a small cell. The hall or maṇḍap has twelve windows of perforated stone, and the *pradakshina* six—two on each side of the shrine.

The columns are all single blocks, and in this and in other temples of the same class in this district, have first, at the bottom, a plain plinth projecting about 1 inch; second, over this, on each face, a raised semicircle (or a little more) filled with sculpture, either of human figures, animals, or flowers; third, up the face of the column a band about nine inches wide, filled with floral tracery; fourth, round the pillar, a deep band of festooned sculpture, in which human and other figures are introduced; and fifth, two bands—one of sculptured human figures and the other of leaves. Above this again is a semicircle filled with figures; but there is considerable variety in the sculptures of the upper portion of the columns. Then comes the massive bracket capital, very deep, and in many cases apparently left unfinished in its details. Every compartment of every pillar is filled with a different sculpture. Plate XL. fig 1. is given as an example of a side of one of the shafts on the north side of the hall. Over the brackets (east and west) lies a heavy beam or lintel of stone, moulded, with horse-shoe-shaped compartments; over this again is another, not quite so wide, divided into compartments by little pilasters; in each compartment is a little temple or cell with horse-shoe-shaped roof—such as we find represented in the Ajaṇṭâ frescoes. Over the pillars of the nave this is doubled, and the roof slopes slightly upwards to this and rests on it. Above this again, in the nave, are deep cross-beams, that have been richly carved on the under sides. The spaces between these beams are covered with slabs which have also been carved; the first, in the nave, is very much damaged and peeled by the water coming through; the second compartment is entirely open; the third has a fine śesha or serpent twined round, with human head and shoulders projecting from the centre (having a five-hooded snake behind), holding up a garland, and on each side is a female or nâginî, with triple hood and the body intertwining with that of the central figure. (See Plate XL. fig. 5.) Lastly, in the compartment just in front of the shrine door is Lakshmî on a triple lotus, with elephants holding the water jars over her. Under the cross-beams in the nave, or central aisle, brackets project, some of them carved into elephants' heads, and in the corners are projecting brackets carved into *siñhas* or lions.

Against the walls, and in line with the columns, are sixteen pilasters, and on the lower part of the shaft of each (except the corner ones) are pairs of figures of various sizes, mostly from three to four and a half feet high, some of them fairly well executed, but many of them much defaced. The females have their hair done up in a sort of arch or half dome, like the snake hood, covering a sort of knob, perhaps representing a gold ornament, the whole reminding one of the way in which the *kasbans* of the south Konkan, about Goa, dress their hair to the present day. This mode may probably be that affected by their ancient sisters, the temple *dasas* or "slaves of the god." A short sword on the right hip of the male figures seems to be a favourite equipment. On the capitals of the pilasters are some wonderful grinning faces, known as *kirtimukhs*—literally "the face of fame."

Along the wall head, over the door and south side of the temple, is a moulded architrave, similar to what is over the pillars, and above it is a carved frieze with little dwarfs carrying a serpentine or undulating roll, similar to what is found at Amravatî (Fergusson's *Tree and Serpent Worship*, p. 187 and Plate LVI.) and elsewhere. On the north side, this last is the lower belt, and a frieze of florid sculpture runs along above it.

PLATE XL.

PAṬṬADKAL - SCULPTURES &c. FROM THE GREAT SAIVA TEMPLE.

1. PILLAR.

D.M. delt.

Scale of [scale bar] Feet

2. BASE

3.

D.M. delt.

4.

5.

PATTADKAL - FACSIMILE OF INSCRIPTIONS FROM THE GREAT TEMPLE.

20 *Size, 2 ft. 2 in. by 1 ft. 8 in.*

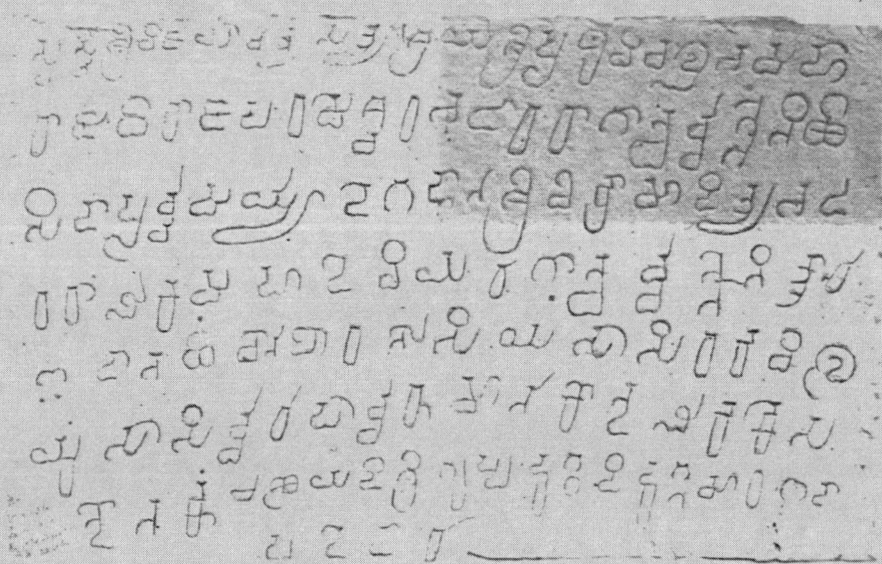

21 *Size, 1 ft. 8 in. by 10 in.*

22

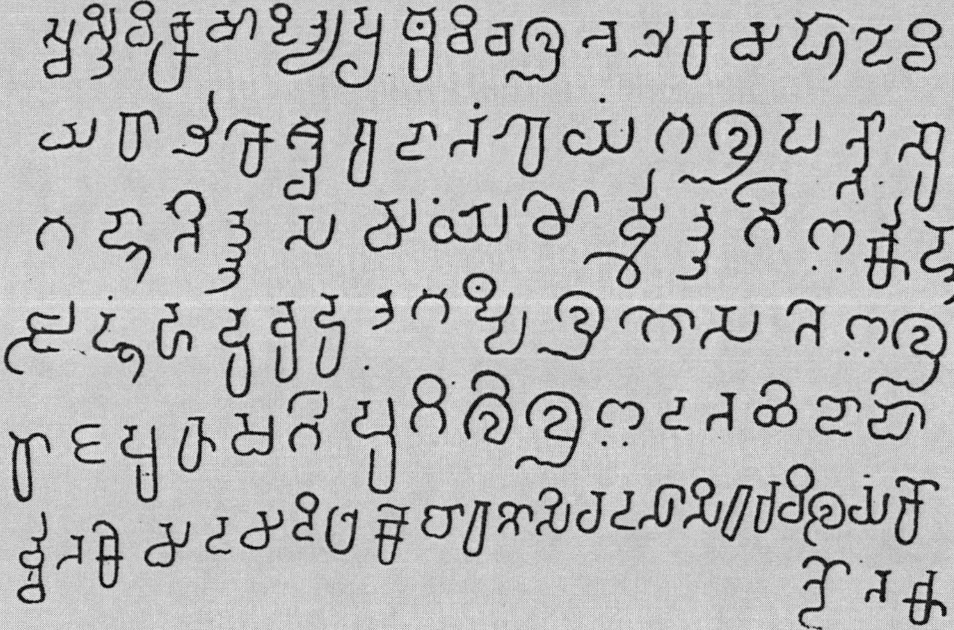

23

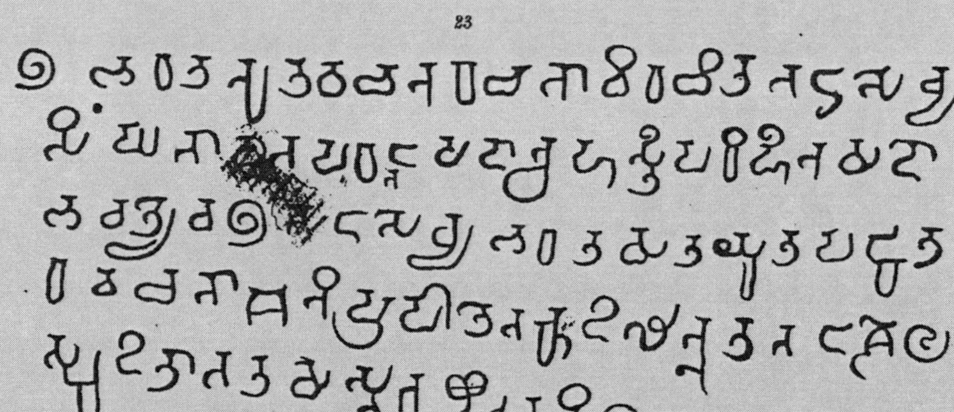

W. Griggs, Photo-lith.

24

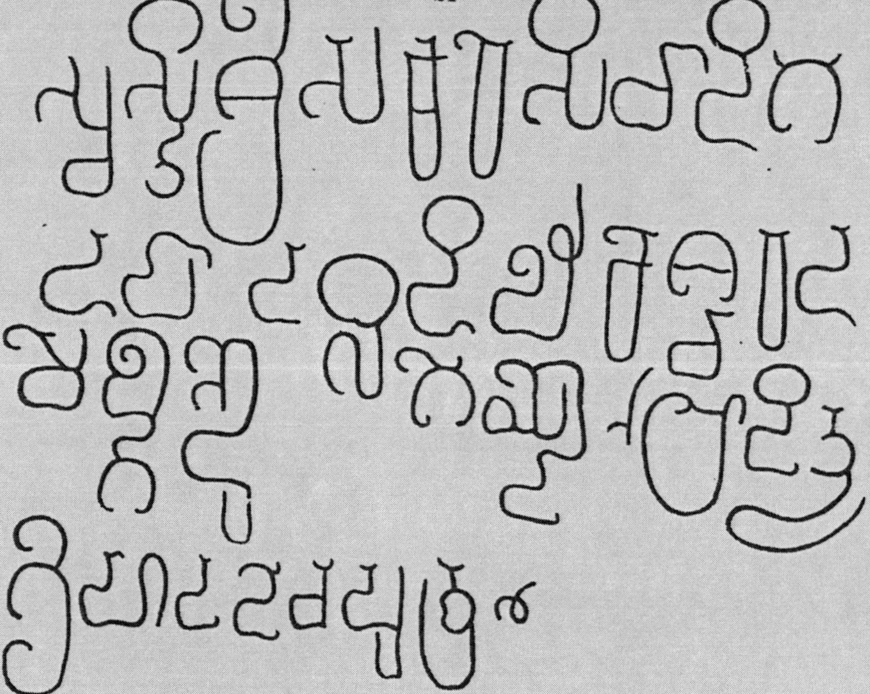

25

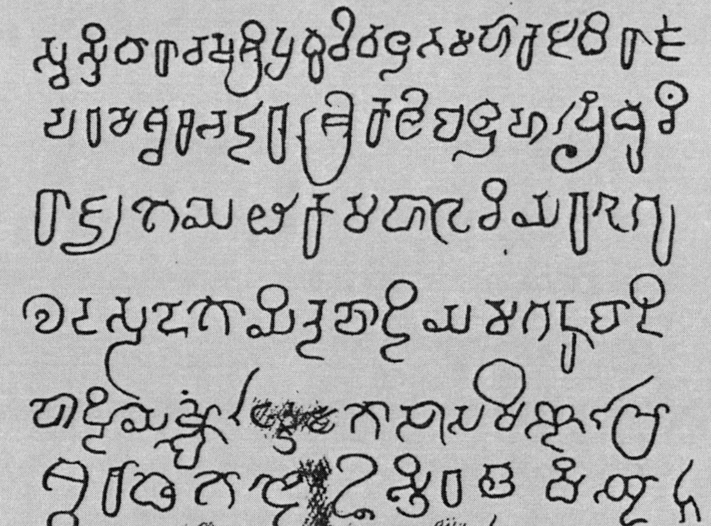

W. Griggs, Photo lith.

26.

27.

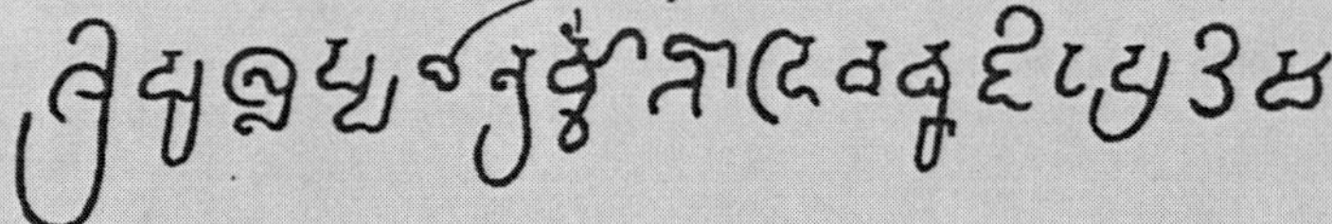

28

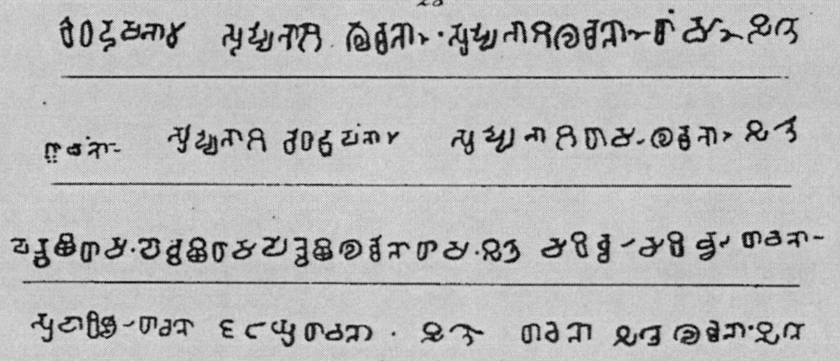

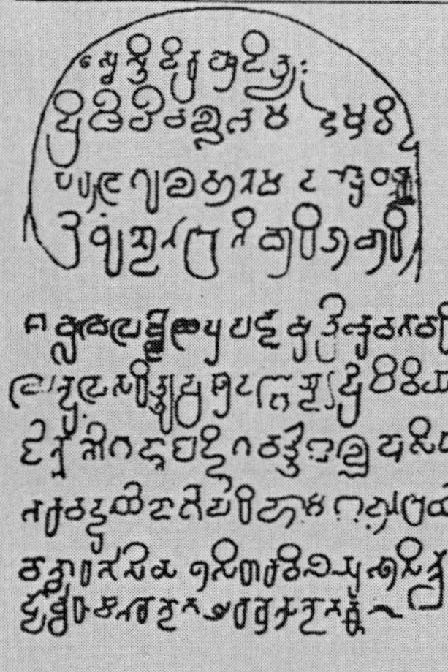

29

W. Griggs, Photo-lith.

On the front of the jambs of the shrine door are groups of female figures. In a small circle on the lintel, surmounted by the horse-shoe canopy, is a figure of Lakshmî, or some other goddess, and above the cornice is another canopy, supported on the shoulders of recumbent females, enclosing a sitting figure with the left knee turned up; but the whole door is besmeared by successive whitewashings, so that the sharpness and distinctness of the sculpture is buried.

The outsides of the walls are covered with sculptures of Vishṇu and Śiva, the latter predominating. Two of these are represented on Plate XL. Fig. 4 is near the south corner of the east face, representing Vishṇu with eight arms (Ashṭabhuja) standing on Garuḍa, with a dwarf, having a grinning face on his belly, standing at his side, while above are a number of capering figures; fig. 3 is at the east end of the north wall and represents Śiva, four armed, with his bull under his foot, and Pârvatî beside him, having her hair dressed in the manner alluded to above. The detail of the base of the temple is given in fig. 2. The stones of the walls are generally immense blocks, closely jointed, without cement.

In a canopy in front of the temple is a colossal Basava or Vṛishabha, the sacred bull, 8 feet 11 inches in length by 6 feet 5½ inches from the platform to the tip of the horn. It is formed of a single block of compact black basalt or porphyry, and in the eyes of the present Lingayat priest and his sect is the principal object of attention.

There are a considerable number of inscriptions about this temple, especially in the east and north porches, but time permitted to copy only a portion of these. (Plates XLI–XLIV.) Some of them were so covered up with whitewash that it was only by the most careful scrutiny they were detected. The characters in which they are cut are all of a type older than the tenth century; and when fully translated they may be expected to throw some light on the date of the temple,—which will probably be found to belong to the eighth century. Inscriptions 20 to 29, and two or three others are all on this building and its gates. Nos. 20 and 21, Plate XLI. are from photographs of the impressions or casts brought away of two inscriptions on the south or left side of the east porch, near the door. Nos. 22 and 23, Plate XLII., are also from the east porch, No. 23 being on the inside of the north front pillar; it is the same as No. XIX. of the *Inscriptions in Dharwar, &c.* It is in Sanskrit verse, and was thus rendered by the late Dr. Bhau Dâjî:—" The elephant, blinded by intoxication (*i.e.* the proud learned) is positively deprived of his inebriety by the lion-sound of delight from the drama composed according to the rules recommended by Bharata,* and the tops (heads) of the mountains, the crooked and proud actors, breaking asunder, fall low indeed by the thunderbolt of the beautiful composition according to the rules of Bharata, as followed by the actors." †

No. 24, Plate XLIII., is over a large sculptured figure on the inside of the west pillar of the north porch.

Inscription 25, Plate XLIII., is on the front pillar in the east porch. It consists of seven lines in Sanskrit and Kanarese, and is regarded by Dr. Bhau Dâji as belonging, with several of the others, to the seventh century; he did not translate it, but made out doubtfully the name of a king as Śrî Kaliballaha, who had the titles of Dhârâvarsha

* Achalada Bharata the author of the *Bharata Sútras.*

† *Jour. Bomb., B.R., Asiat. Soc.* Vol. IX. p. 320.

Śrî Prithivi Vallabha mahârâjadhirâja parameśvara Bhattâraka', and whom he thought might perhaps be one of the Râshtrakuta dynasty.

No. 26, on Plate XLIV., is a tracing from an inscription under a figure of Śiva on the south wall of the temple. Śiva is represented with very bushy hair and his left foot on the back of a dwarf figure. No. 27 is a copy of another over a figure of Śiva near the west end of the north face of the temple. The next, No. 28, is reduced from a tracing of the inscription photographed as No. XVIII. of the *Inscriptions in Dharwar*, where it is photographed to a scale of less than 1¾ inch to 2 feet. It consists of four lines inserted on narrow facias between belts of sculpture on the face of a pillar on the south side of the nave of the temple, and is evidently explanatory of the sculpture, which represents scenes from the *Râmâyaṇa*. The first line reads "Karadûśana,* Suppa Nâgi,† "Lakkanâ, Suppanâgi, Lakkanâ.‡ Râma. Sîte." The second, "Ravana. Suppanâgi, "Karadûśana. Suppanâgi, Rama. Lakkanâ. Sîte." The third, "Pollathi,§ Râma. "Pollathi, Râma, Pollathi, Lakkanâ, Râma, Sîte Maricha.‖ Maricha. Râvaṇa." And the fourth, "Suppanâgi (?) Râvaṇa. Jaṭâyu, Ravâṇa. Sîte, Râvaṇa, Site, Lakkanâ, Sîte."

No. 29, is from an imperfect impression of an inscription on the north side of the entrance gate. It is much abraded in some parts and difficult to copy. There is a similar one on the south side, but a rubble wall has been built against it, and time and means were wanting to attempt taking impressions of it.

In a hut, to the north of the temple, is an octagonal pillar, with high square base, on seven sides of which is a long inscription, 3 feet 10 inches in depth, with twenty-five lines of 8 inches long on each side, and eight lines more on the east face of the base,—some of them partially peeled off. It was impossible from the heat and stench, even in the early morning, to attempt copying it. The part of the hut in which it stands is that allotted to the buffaloes, and the pillar would require to be removed to the open air and carefully washed with caustic potash, to secure a fair copy; it may be of some historical importance and ought to be preserved.

I was unable, from an accident to my silver bath, to take any photographs here, but there is a series of photographic views of the temples at Paṭṭadkal in the volume published in 1866 of *Architecture in Dharwar and Mysore*. Plate LIV. in that volume represents the south-west portion of this temple; Plate LV. (of which Plate XXXVIII. here is a reduced copy) is the south-east portion, excluding the front; Plate LVI. is the front taken from the same point; and Plate LVII., the temple from the east-south-east with a portion of the Nandi pavilion.

On the north-west of the great temple is another exactly similar in plan and most of its details. It appears in Plates LIX. and LX. of the *Architecture in Dharwar, &c.* It is now occupied by cows and the family owning them, who are blackening it with the smoke of their cooking, and otherwise injuring it, and as they have no claim to the temple, they might as well be turned out of it.

The pillars are 2 feet 4 inches to 2 feet 5 inches square, and sculptured similarly to those in the great temple. Five of those in the nave have human figures in the central

* Kharadûśana—two brothers of Tadakâ, giants.

† Sûrpa Nakhâ—a sister of the giant Râvaṇa, having long and broad nails.

‡ Lakshmana—the brother of Râma.

§ Paulastya or Râvaṇa, or simply a Râkshasa or descendant of Pulastya.

‖ Mâricha, a Râkshasa slain by Râma. The scenes evidently refer to the legend of Sûrpa Nakhâ, related in Talboys Wheeler's *Hist. of India*, Vol. II. chap. 16.

compartment of the bracket capitals. In the compartment of the roof in front of the shrine is Lakshmî and the elephants, with flying figures round. This figure—so often referred to, and here occurring on a very old temple—may perhaps be taken as, on the whole, indicating that the building where it occurs is ancient.* In the next compartment is Śesha again, with his hands clasped, a figure which, with the square massive pillars and other distinctive characteristics, connects these temples with the age of the Badâmi caves. The third is open; the fourth compartment has Śiva dancing, attended by his consort Umâ or Pârvatî and his bull; and the fifth, like the third, has lost its roof. The roof of the shrine is carved with the lotus and arabesques, and around the wall head are floating and dancing figures.

This old Dravidian temple is more weatherworn than the other, and on the whole, I think, it is probably the older of the two, but if so, not by above half a century. The length inside from the entrance to the shrine door is 47 feet, the width 39 feet 4 inches. And at a short distance in front of it is the remains of a gateway. It ought surely to be conserved from wilful destruction, from smoke, and from cowdung, &c., and might be utilized as a store for inscriptions and pieces of sculpture.

Besides the temples in the Dravidian style, Paṭṭadkal also possesses a group of temples, not remarkable for their size or architectural beauty, but interesting because they exhibit the two principal styles of Indian architecture in juxta-position, as is elsewhere the case only at Bhavâneśvar in Orissa. Close to the north side of the temple last described is a smaller one, the spire of which is of the northern Hindu style, but the details and ornamentation of the temple are Dravidian, indicating perhaps that, though intended as an imitation of the style of northern India, the workmen were Kanarese and were left to finish the detail to the best of their ability. Like all the temples here of the northern style, the maṇḍap or hall is small, supported by only four columns, and corresponding pilasters. There is a good deal of carving on the roof, the pillars, and the door of the shrine. On the fronts of four of the pilasters are carved mythological siñhas or lions with horns, while against the columns have been human figures: three of the pillars have capitals similar to what we find in Cave XXIV at Ajaṇṭâ, in the Viśvâkarma Cave, and in a more ornate form in the Tîn Tâl Cave at Elora, with a thick circular torus over which foliage hangs at the corners. The shafts are of the rather unusual form of duodecagons. The maṇḍap measures 17 feet 8 inches wide by 11 feet 2 inches. The shrine is 8 feet 4 inches deep by 9 feet 7 inches wide; the whole length of the temple inside the walls being 32 feet 3 inches. On the roof of the shrine is a lotus, and the cornice is dentilated.

A few yards north from this is a cell with a *linga*,—a mere fragment of a temple, of which the stones have been carried away for buildings about the village.

About thirty yards north-east from this last is a large temple in the Dravidian style. Some of the figures in the compartments of the walls outside have never been finished. The front of the maṇḍap (if ever it was closed) is gone; but probably it was always open on this side. It has six columns in depth, square blocks with outlines of carving chipped out, similar in pattern to that on the pillars of the great temple: the roof and architraves under it and the door of shrine are perfectly plain. At the entrance is a fine śilaśâśana

* Vide ante, p. 13.

or slab with a long inscription, quite unprotected from the buffaloes rubbing against it. This is the temple appearing on the left of the following woodcut.

A few yards north of this is a small shrine with an outer chamber, of which the roof is gone : carried off, like many more, for building purposes.

North of this again is a large spire with white *kalas* or finial, and part of the *pradakshiná* of a temple in the northern style. The remainder has been carried off.

Behind, or to the west of this last, and on the present wall of the village, is another spire, also in the Northern style, with the usual small chamber that does service for a *maṇḍap* or hall in these temples, and of which the roof in this case has been carried away. On a large stone, on the east face of the spire, is a sculpture of Śiva dancing, with Pârvatî and Nandi.

The annexed view of this temple and of the last-mentioned Draviḍian one, borrowed from the *Architecture of Dharwar and Mysore,* " places the two forms," as Mr. Fergusson remarks, " in vivid contrast. The building on the left is a storeyed pyramid of Draviḍian architecture; on the right a tower in the northern style. In this style, as in the other, the base is generally of a cubical form, but in the north with a slight projection on each face. The upper part, at its springing, somewhat overhangs the base. Above this it is generally perpendicular at first, but always falling inwards with a gentle curve towards the summit. The most marked characteristic is that its outline is never rectilinear, and it is never divided into storeys as in the southern style. Above the part square in section, the tower is crowned by a melon-shaped feature called the *amla śila.* In Orissa it is flat and broad. In the example last quoted it is more closely assimilated to the domical form of the southern style, though still in reality perfectly distinct."*

Outside the wall and a few yards to the north, in the field once covered with temples, is another small temple in the northern style, from which the roof of the *maṇḍap* has also been carried off.

---

* *Architecture of Dharwar and Mysore*, p. 43.

1. PLAN.

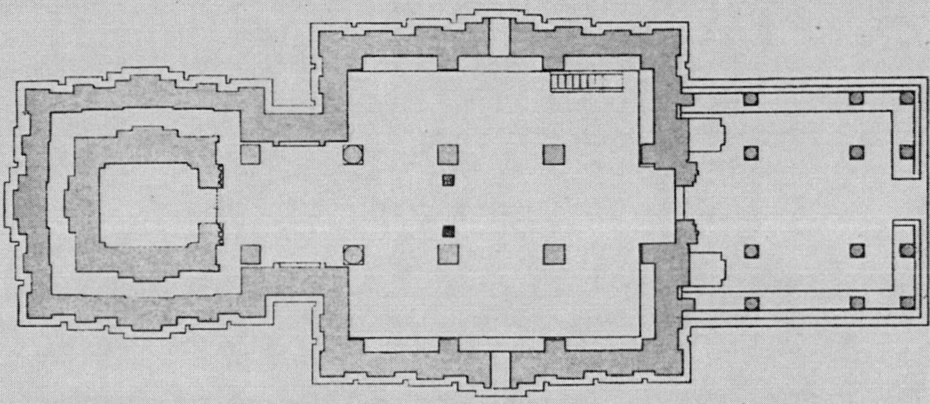

J. Burgess, delt.

2.

3.

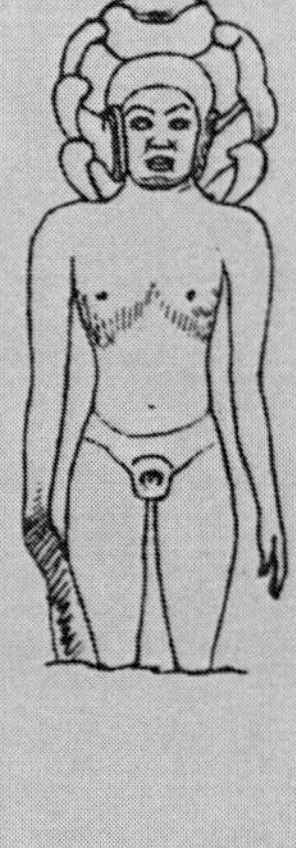

PLATE XLVI.

PAṬṬADKAL - TEMPLE OF PÂPANÂTHA.

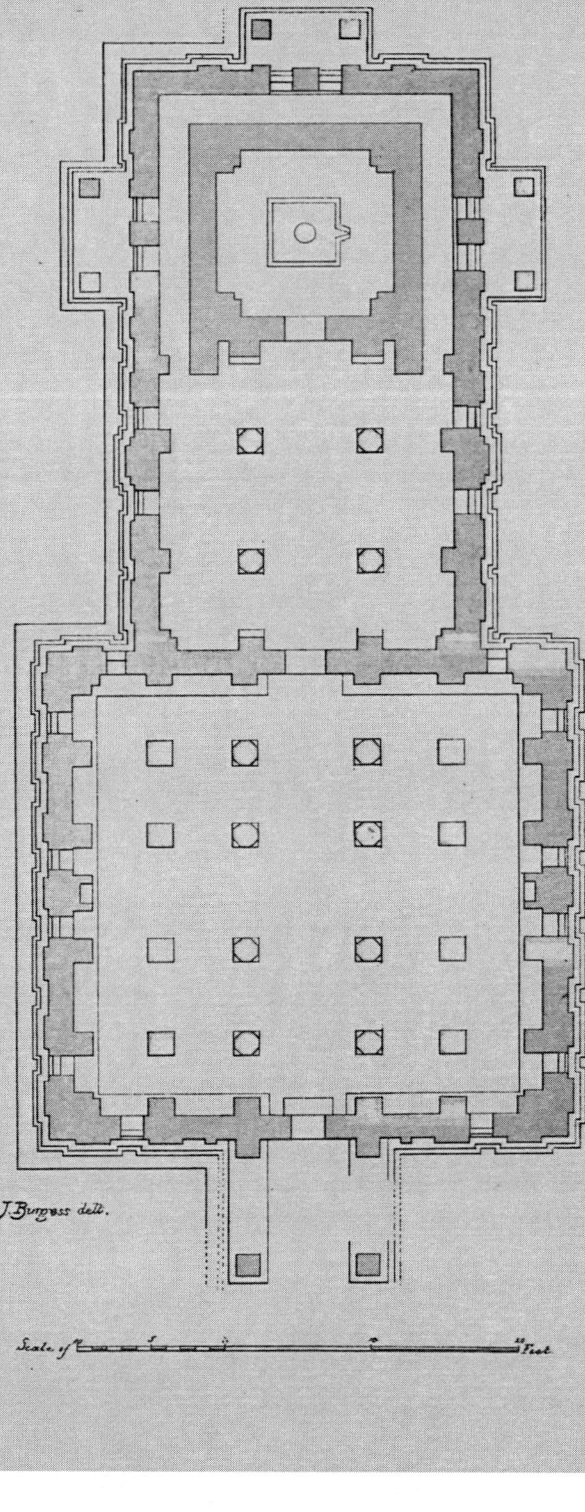
J. Burgess delt.
Scale of Feet

1. PLAN OF THE JAINA CAVE.

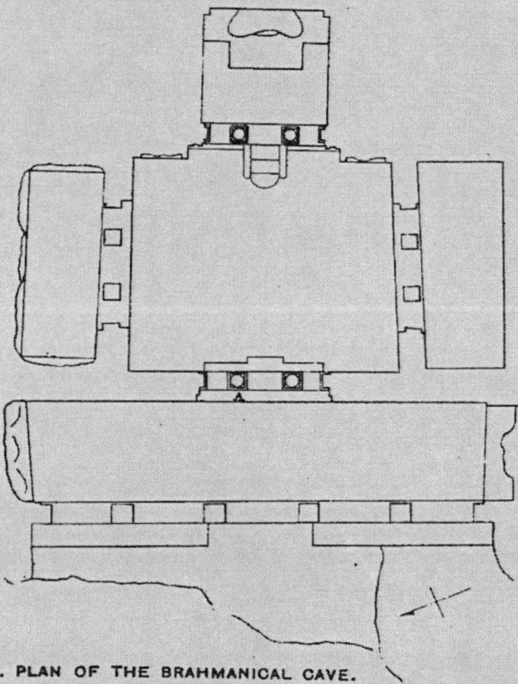

2.
COLUMN A.

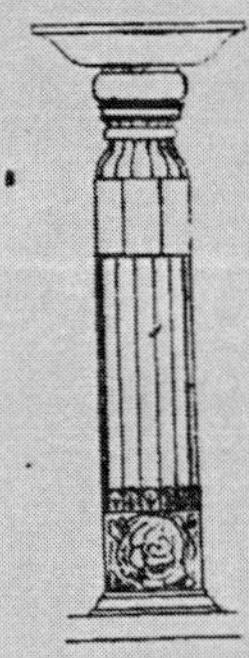

3. PLAN OF THE BRAHMANICAL CAVE.

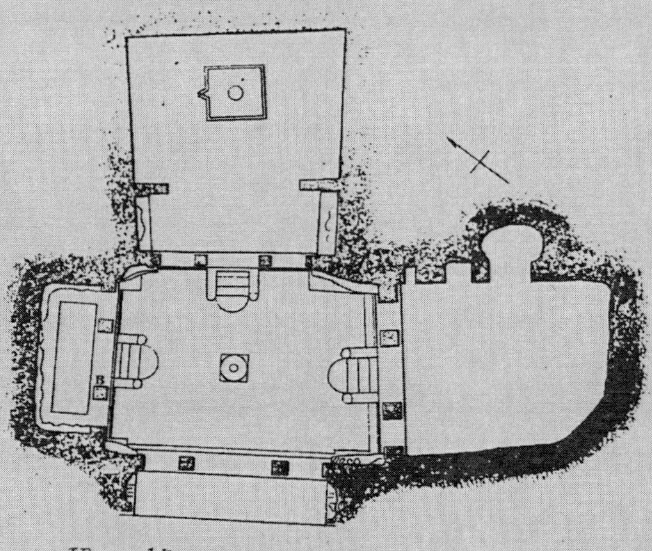

4
COLUMN. B.

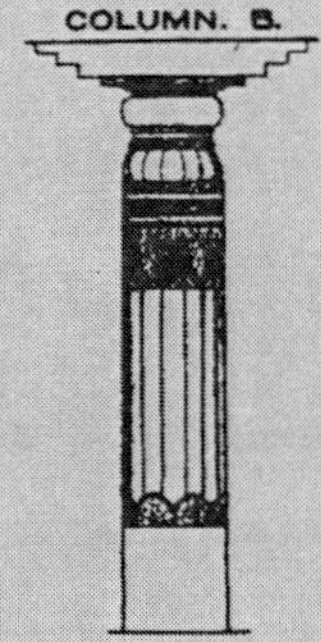

J. Burgess. delt.

In all these old Saiva temples, the free introduction of figures of Vishṇu and other Vaishṇava emblems is very observable. The Lingâyat reform in these provinces in the twelfth century must, in one aspect, have been a protest against the Vaishṇava element in the religion; and we find accordingly that the *Lingayat Purâṇas* speak anything but respectfully of Vishṇu. (See *Jour. Bomb. B. R. As. Soc.*, vol. viii. pp. 142, 163, 164, 179.)

Proceeding north-west across the field, in which several of the lingas of old temples have been left standing, we come to six very massive square pillars with one cross lintel, and in line with them, a little to the west, four others, and then a linga—evidently all parts of one large temple. The pillars have been elaborately carved, and some of the sculpture is still pretty sharp, but obscene. In this field are also two monumental stones worth preserving.

West of this, and in another field is an old Jaina temple, built in the Dravidian style, see Plate XLV. It has an open maṇḍap 20 feet 3 inches long and 19 feet wide inside, supported by eight pillars and two pilasters on the screen, and by four slender columns about 9 feet 4 inches apart on the floor. On each side of the door is the front half of an elephant, with a rider, reaching nearly to the roof;—the rider on the right side is canopied by a five-hooded snake. The door has only floral ornaments round it, and below the outer architrave on each side is a fat sitting figure in bas-relief; at the base of the inner moulding is a flower-pot or water-jar. The outside of the ledge round this manḍap is ornamented with sculptures of water-jars, siñhas or lions, and figures like the gaṇa found on Śaiva temples. The inner *manḍap* or temple proper, is 30 feet 8 inches long by 32 feet 3 inches wide, supported by four square pillars 8 feet 7 inches apart, and by corresponding heavy pilasters. The columns have a very heavy torus, and the height of the temple may have been about 12 feet 3 inches, but the floor is much filled up with rubbish.

The antechamber measures about 13 feet 4 inches square, and has two round pillars in front, set well into the temple, and two square ones, 8 feet 10 inches apart, in front of the shrine. The shrine door is plainly moulded, except the florid *makaras* on each end of the lintel (see Plate XLV. fig. 2.) on the heads of the slender colonnettes of the jambs. The shrine is 9 feet 9 inches wide by 8 feet 11 inches deep, and is now empty. A figure of a man—probably Parśvanâtha—lies in the temple broken. (See Fig. 3.)

There is a stone ladder in the north-east corner of the hall leading up to the roof, which has fallen in in several places; and a lintel which has given way has been supported by two small pillars. Round the shrine is a narrow *pradakshina* or passage for circumambulation, and in the tower above is a chamber. The outside is very plain, with small figures of *Jinas* or *Siddhas*, *devîs*, elephants, &c., on the finials and gargoyles —some of the latter being very curious. The temple faces east, and has an opening or window on the north and south sides.

At the south-east corner of the village, partly on the wall, and long deserted for purposes of worship, is the temple of Pâpanâtha—one of the oldest now remaining at Paṭṭadkal, and used by some of the villagers living near it to house their cattle in. It is represented in the photographic Plate XLVI. and the plan on Plate XLVII. With no note or tradition, with nothing but the Photograph of the exterior to guide him, it is not to be wondered that Mr. Fergusson, in 1866, was inclined to ascribe this and the other temples here to a comparatively modern date. I could hear of no tradition on the spot, indeed the villagers seemed to have no traditions unconnected with the Lingayat sect: the inscriptions did not look promising, though some of them might perhaps yield the name of a Châlukya king or even a date; but from a comparison of its style with that of the others, and from the details of sculpture and interior arrangement, I feel strongly inclined to regard this as one of the oldest structural temples yet examined, though possibly others of the same age may exist hereabouts or at Aiwaḷḷi.

It has been elaborately finished in the northern or Bengal style, and still retains some remarkable perforated windows, with snakes, lions, &c., wrought into the different patterns. The sculptures outside are illustrative of the *Râmâyaṇa*, and the monkeys, Râma, Sîtâ, Jatayus, Râvaṇa, &c., are frequent figures, with the names engraved against each, as in the sculptures of the tope at Bharahut,* and in characters of about the fifth century.

On the roof inside are two Śeshas and other figures, and in the corners of each compartment are brackets carved as siñhas in entire relief; in the porch two of them have elephant heads. The inner lines of pillars are octagons, the outer square, and each of the pillars of the nave, has a female figure in alto-rilievo in front of the shaft; but the first pillar on the left has a pair, and the pilasters have a pair each. The bracket capitals are large and heavy. There is next, an inner temple, of which the columns are very plain. Round the shrine is a very narrow *pradakshina*, with windows on each side. On the lintel of the shrine is a flying figure, probably Garuḍa, with a sword in each hand. High up above it is Lakshmî and the elephants, with a flying figure on each side coming out of a *makara's* mouth; and over this a row of figures.

In the compartment of the roof, just before the shrine, is a Śesha with flying figures in the corners; in the next is Śiva dancing, with Pârvatî beside him; and the cross-beam between the compartments is minutely carved.

On the lintel of the door, from the outer to the inner maṇḍap, is a flying Garuḍa —also a conclusive proof that this temple, like most of the other early Châlukya shrines, was Vaishṇava. The compartment of the roof next to this door has a figure of Lakshmî, with a wonderfully rich border of male and female flying figures; the second has a fine Śesha with nâginîs at the corners; the third has a Nâga Râja in the centre, standing (or dancing ?) with a figure mounted on a buffalo at his left hand, and another on a horse at his right, while above and below these, on three small panels, are figures riding on various animals. The roofs of these compartments are higher than the rest, and the cross-beams are neatly carved and supported by *siñha* brackets. On the architrave or lintel over the pillars are horse-shoe-shaped niches surrounding heads, as on the façade of Cave I. at Ajantâ and elsewhere, and above these are small representations in bas-relief of Draviḍian shrines and other ornamentation.

The frieze all round the wall head is carved with dwarf figures supporting a rope or roll of flowers, similar to that already referred to at Amravatî (Fergusson's *Tree and Serpent Worship*, Plate LVI., and p. 187).

In a niche or recess in the north wall, inside, is a figure of Maheśvara, and opposite to it on the south side another of Gaṇeśa or Gaṇapati.

---

* *Indian Antiquary*, Vol. III. p. 256.

AIWALLI - PORTION OF CARVING ON THE ROOF OF VERANDA - JAINA CAVE.

Burgess delt.

AIWALLI.

The caves at Aiwalli—the *Iwullee* and *Eiwally* of the older maps,—have scarcely ever been noticed. The first mention of them seems to be in a letter of 11th December 1851, from Mr. W. (now Sir Walter) Elliot, M.C.S., to the Bombay Government. The Bombay Asiatic Society promised to publish the letter, but never did so; and the notice of it in the Society's Proceedings* merely states that "it makes mention of some caves "not noticed in Dr. Wilson's Memoir, viz., at Badami; Eiwally, a village on the banks "of the Malpurba; and at the village of Undavalli, on the banks of the Krishna." Beyond this I have met with no other published mention of these caves. They are two in number, both small, at some distance from one another, and one Jaina the other Brahmanical.

On Monday 13th April, I began the examination of the remains at Aiwalli with the Jaina Cave. It is in the face of a rocky hill, west-south-west from the village, and north-east from the group of old temples on the rocky bank of the river. The cave faces south-south-west, and in front of the four pillars of the verandah, a wall has been built of three courses of large hewn stones, 1 foot 7 inches thick—some of the twelve stones forming it containing as much as twenty-four, and one nearly twenty-nine cubic feet. The space between the middle pair of columns 4 ft. 9 in. wide and 6 ft. 11 in. high, is left open for the entrance.

The verandah is about 32 feet in length, 7 feet 3 inches wide, and 8 feet 3 inches high, and the roof of it is sculptured in bas-relief with *makaras*, frets, and flowers. A portion of it, the width of the verandah, is represented, Plate XLIX. At the left end of this apartment is Pârśvanâtha Śeshaphaṇi, or "with the Sesha hood," as at Badâmi, only the sculpture here has been quite finished; the male and female on his right have each a snake-hood, and illustrate how closely the early Jaina sculpture followed and copied the forms of the Bauddha. At the other end of the verandah is a figure of a Jina or Nâtha, as at Badâmi, with two female supporters, and behind him is a tree with two figures among the branches to his left.

By a door, 8 ft. wide and 6 ft. 5 in. high, divided by two small pillars (see plan, Plate XLVIII. fig. 1, and drawing of one of these pillars, fig. 2), we enter the hall or *shâla*, about 15 feet deep by 17 feet 8 inches wide, and 7 feet 11 inches high. The roof has a large lotus in the centre, depending about 6 inches, and four others, one between each corner and the centre, projecting 2 or 2½ inches from the level; the interspaces are filled up with makaras, fishes, flowers, and human heads springing out of arabesque tracery.

At the back of the hall, on the right side, is a dwârapâla with a lofty head-dress, and frill behind it, as at Elephanta, holding a lotus in his hand, attended by a curly-headed dwarf or Piśâcha with a fish, and who has a long earring in one ear and a round one in the other. On the left side is a similar dwârapâla with a female dwarf holding some roundish object. Up three or four steps, entered by a triple doorway, 5 feet 6 inches high is the shrine, about 8 feet 2 inches square, and 8 feet 5 inches high, with a sitting figure of the Tîrthañkara, very similar to the one at Badâmi. On the front of the *Asana* or throne, are some letters; but, from want of time and light, I could not make them out: many of them seemed to be illegible.

---

* *Jour. Bomb. B. R. Asiat. Soc.* Vol. IV. p. 460.

Right and left of the hall are two cells, little over 5 feet deep, about 14 feet long, and 6 feet 5 inches high, entered by triple doors separated by pillars. That on the right side is perfectly plain, the other is covered on the three walls with sculpture, apparently never quite finished. In the middle of the back wall is Mahâvîra, the twenty-fourth Tîrthañkara, with three lions on his throne, and *chauṅri*-bearers with high caps standing behind. On Mahâvîra's right, below, is the head and shoulders of a figure in the act of adoration, with a five-hooded snake over the head; and on the other side is a female with a single snake-hood behind her head-dress. Behind the male head and round the return of the wall are about a dozen people; a pair on the end wall are sitting on the ground with *chauṅri*-bearers behind them. On the other side are the same number, three of them on (or behind) an elephant on the end wall; but some of the figures in this chamber are merely blocked out, and scarcely any are quite finished.

The pillars in front of this and the corresponding chamber on the other side are square, without bases, and with only a rough capital or small bracket. There has been a wooden door to shut the triple entrance into the hall, hung inside the pillars.

On the rock or hill above this cave are many dolmens or cromlechs: a large number are standing, but all I could visit want the ends; in one case, however, the stone, with a hole in it, lies beside the dolmen. Some are full of earth, whether brought in by white ants or only taken possession of by them, is perhaps uncertain. They seemed larger than those at Konur; one side stone measured 11 feet 9 inches, and the areas were proportionally large, but they are not high.

West from the cave, and near the foot of the hill, are two old shrines; one with two plain square columns inside; and the other, with three doors, has, on its east side, two Śaiva commemorative slabs with a good deal of carving on them. But the Wadâris seem to have been recently at work here as elsewhere about Aiwaḷḷi.

The Brahmanical cave is to the north-west of Aiwaḷḷi, and faces south-west by west. (See photograph Plate L., and plan, Plate XLVIII., 3.) It has two plain square pillars in front, within which is the hall, 18 feet 7 inches wide by 13 feet 5 inches deep, and 8 feet 9 inches high. On each side the entrance is a dwârapâla—weatherworn to obliteration of all but the outlines; and outside are fat sitting figures, represented in a sort of shrine, also weatherworn.

Five steps above the level of the hall is the antechamber, which appears to have been separated from the shrine beyond, by a neatly carved door, *built* in, but now fallen, the lintel and one jamb still lying inside. The depth of the antechamber and shrine together is about 15½ feet by 14 feet wide, the antechamber being 6 feet 10 inches high, and the shrine 7 feet 4 inches. On each side the hall is a chamber. They have each two pillars (Plate XLVIII. 4) and two pilasters in front, and are raised by four or five steps above the floor of the hall; that on the right, about 12 feet wide by 14 feet deep, is quite unfinished, but may originally have been like the other, and afterwards enlarged. On the back wall of the left one is a ten-armed Śiva dancing. On his left is a small figure, the head of it gone, then Pârvatî, and on the end of the chamber a Kinnarâ or horse-headed female—one of the choristers of Kailâs or Śiva's heaven, and two female dancers—the one on the extreme right with a skull on the *mugut* or high head-dress. On Śiva's right is, first, Gaṇapati eating *ladus* or balls of sweetmeat, his favourite food; then a dancing female; then high up in the corner, the skeleton of Śiva's devotee

Bringi; and lastly, on the end wall, three female figures—the middle one Pârvatî or Chandî, with the crescent moon on her *mugut*, while the outer one holds a *mâlâ* or rosary and something like a bottle. All have very high head-dresses, and the females very deep bracelets.

In the hall between the front of this chamber and the left pilaster of the entrance to the cave is a figure of Arddhanâri, the androgynous, or conjoint male *and* female form of Śiva, with a long *triśula* or trident, holding her hair in her hand, a deep anklet on her leg, and the crescent on the high cap. Below is a tiger and Piśâcha, or dwarf.

At the south corner is Śiva and Pârvatî with Bringi. Out of Siva's cap rise three female heads, representative of Gañgâ, Yamunâ, and Sarasvatî,—or Umâ, Lakshmî, and Sarasvatî,—the female triad.* Below these figures are four *gaṇa*,—Bringi in the attitude of supplicating, one holding a cobra, a third the *triśula*, and the fourth, with a high cap, seated European fashion, next the door.

In the north corner, is a male figure with battle axe and triśula, holding up a cobra by the tail in his right hand; over his left shoulder hangs a chain which descends to his feet. Below, on a little square projection, is a sitting dwarf, and beside it a smaller large-bellied one standing and eating (or blowing a reed ?).

On the other side of the entrance to the shrine, in the east corner, are a pair of figures. They are dressed nearly alike, both have the chain depending to the feet; Śiva or Hara has only two arms, with the right holding his *triśula*, round the head of which twines a cobra,—but the shaft, as well as his left hand, has been broken within a few years back. The other figure has four hands (as Vishṇu is often represented); in the right he holds up a cobra and a small rosary, and in one of the left his *śankha* or war conch; he has a crescent on the right side of his *mugut*, of which the sides differ so markedly as, with the third eye in the forehead, to indicate that this was intended for Harihara, the conjoint form of Śiva and Vishṇu. Between the figures another cobra twines round the head of what may be intended for an ensign. Below are four musical *gaṇa*. These last three groups were photographed, but owing to the want of light, and the intense dry heat, the negatives are very thin.

On the base, below the cell and to the right of these last, are three *gaṇa* on each side of the steps, all except one, lying kicking or tumbling.

On the floor is a lotus rising 8 inches above the level. The ceiling is neatly sculptured in the style of the Jaina cave, with a large lotus flower in the centre, and round it a border of flowers in squares, set diagonally. Outside this is a plain band 6 inches wide, then a second belt of lotus flowers and human heads with arabesque continuations.

In the approach to the shrine are two sculptures; on the left hand Varâha—the boar incarnation of Vishṇu with Prithvî, or the personification of the Earth, supported on his hand, and below Śesha and Śeshâ; on the right is Mahiśâsurî slaying the buffalo-demon Mahiśa, and attended by her tiger. The roof of this portion has a lotus in the centre, and a medallion on each side, one with Vishṇu on Garuḍa, and two figures with offerings: the other has a male and female on an elephant, and three other figures. The cell is quite plain and contains only a *chavaranga* or altar.

* See my *Elephanta*, § 44.

Outside this cave, on each side, there is a small temple overgrown with prickly pear. On the roof of that to the west is Vishṇu with a snake-hood, attended by females. In front, and about 30 yards from the cave, is a high monolith with sixteen flutes, the top of it destroyed. (See photograph, Plate L.)

North-west from the cave is an old temple with a *pradakshina* round the shrine. On the roof of the porch is Kârttikeya on his peacock, with a lance and surrounding figures. Inside is a fine śilaśâśanam, and on the north side of the front or west face of the temple is an ancient inscription in five very long lines, the upper somewhat damaged, and the whole weatherworn, and requiring the light to fall across it at a very low angle to render it legible. Over the door of the shrine is a figure of Garuḍa—proving it to have been a Vaishṇava fane, as it has been already remarked, so many of the earlier Châlukya temples in these districts are.

Beside this temple are two small shrines and much *débris*. In front is a *Wâv* or well, with a descent to the water by steps, but it is now disused and partially filled up. A few yards further to the south-west lies an old Jaina statue, much weatherworn. From this or some similar image hereabouts, Colonel Biggs' Photograph No. IV. of an inscription of two lines, was taken. It states, according to Dr. Bhâu Dâji,* "that Râma Setti (*merchant*) of Mûla Sangha Balâtkhâra-gaṇa, caused a 'nisidi' (house of rest) to be constructed."

Near it are five commemorative slabs, from which the inscriptions are rapidly disappearing. At the south-west gate of Aiwaḷḷi, two large carved slabs have been built into the modern wall, and are now very much worn by cattle, &c. rubbing against them. Two others in better preservation stand near by, awaiting destruction when required to repair a house or a byre, or even a fence.

In an old temple in a field south-west from the village is an inscription (No. 33, Plate LV.) in four lines very clearly cut on a pilaster in the south side of the porch. It was taken by Colonel Biggs on a scale of $1\frac{7}{10}$ by $1\frac{1}{2}$ inches (*Inscriptions in Dharwar*, &c. No. VII.), and is considered by the late Dr. Bhâu Dâji † as a Sanskṛit verse, "written about the seventh century of the Christian era," and rendered thus:—

"Peace. No man so skilful in the construction of houses and temples as Marsobha lived, or ever will live, in Jambudvîpa."

On the north side of the porch is the inscription No. 34, not quite so distinct.

On the roof of the porch is Śiva dancing, while Pârvatî holds a child—perhaps Kârttikeya. Over both the door to the maṇḍap and that of the shrine, Garuḍa is figured, and over the entrance also Lakshmî and the elephants. The roof has been torn off the temple. The pillars are plain square shafts, but the architrave over them in the nave is sculptured with frolicing gaṇa, some in obscene attitudes. This temple appears to be about the same age as the Durga temple, to be noticed next.

The little information we had hitherto been able to obtain respecting the curious temple on the north-east outskirts of the village, and locally known as the "Durga," was most unsatisfactory. It was spoken of as a Jaina temple, and sometimes as a Śaiva one, and was supposed to be the one on which was the important inscription of A.D. 584 to which I have already alluded. As the only known example of its class

---

* *Jour. Bom. B. R. As. Soc.* Vol. IX. p. 315.

† Ibid., p. 316.

AIWAḶḶI - BRAHMANICAL CAVE.

PLATE LI.

AIWAḶḶI – THE DURGA TEMPLE.

as a structural building, it is to the Indian antiquary one of the most interesting temples in the south of India. It was therefore a special object of attention with me. I could find no inscription containing a date upon it, but the style of the interior is so closely allied to that of Cave III. at Badâmi that it was evident it must be placed within a century after the cave. The plan, with the round apse (see Plate LII.), is unique, and suggests that it might represent a Buddhist Chaitya structural temple. In the absence of plans, however, or any detailed description, all we could previously conjecture was that the apse was a representation of what a Buddhist Chaitya like that at Karlê would have been had it been a free-standing structural building.

Either the roof had fallen in or been destroyed—most likely the latter, and the Marâṭhas of a century or two ago piled up a wall of rubble masonry round the roof and formed a ramp round the spire, utilizing it as a keep and watch-tower. The interior also is half filled with stones and rubbish. It might be cleaned out, and cattle prevented from entering it as they now do, while the aisles might be used for storing some of the many sculptured and inscribed slabs that lie about waiting destruction.

VAISHAṆVA TEMPLE AT AIWAḶḶI.

The accompanying woodcut from *Architecture of Dharwar and Mysore* (p. 67), represents the apse of this temple from the south-west, and the photograph (Plate LI.) is a view taken from the north-east.

Architecturally, as remarked by Mr. Fergusson in 1866, it was "not so important to which religion it was originally dedicated as it is to know what its interior arrangements may have been, and the light which an examination of it would throw on the whole subject of cave architecture would be so great that there are few temples in India that would more fully repay a careful and detailed illustration."

I regretted that the rain forced me to leave Aiwaḷḷi sooner than I had intended and prevented my making so full a survey of this and other temples here as they seemed to require. The temple was neither Jaina nor Śaiva, but a genuine Châlukya temple of

Vishṇu. The plan (Plate LII.) will show the size and general arrangements, which need not be more particularly noted here. In the wall of the temple inside the surrounding portico are nine niches in which are mythological figures of Nṛisiñha, Maheśâsurî, Varâha, Vishṇu, Arddhanâri, Śiva, &c. Between the niches are six perforated stone windows—four belonging to the aisles of the temple, and two to the *pradakshina;* and below the level of these is a belt of sculpture consisting of mythological scenes, *gaṇa*, arabesques, &c. Two of the gaṇa are represented on Plate LII. figs. 2 and 3. Of the twenty-eight original columns that surround it, twelve in front have sculptures—a pair of figures on the outer sides: otherwise these pillars are plain square blocks. The sketch, Plate LII. fig. 4, represents the figures on the front of the left hand pillar at the entrance. The four pillars of the inner porch are more elaborate: besides the larger pairs of figures on the outer sides, they have a band of *gaṇa* near the bottom; farther up the shaft a medallion, usually with three figures; and above this again a deep belt with arabesque drapery below and *gaṇa* above, crowned with a fillet of leaves; and on the neck of the column, resting on this, is another medallion with small figures (photograph, Plate LIII.). The brackets over the shaft are not much carved. The ten pillars of the hall of the temple are very similar to those of the porch; and the roof is raised by a deep architrave—a sort of triforium in fact—four feet in height, above the brackets, and further by about one foot, by the cross-beams. The shrine, which occupies the place of the *dahgoba* in Bauddha Cave temples, has a *pradakshina* round it, and is semicircular at the back.

The door of the temple is richly carved, reminding us of the elaborate doorways at Ajaṇṭâ, and the carving is continued up to the very roof, 4 feet 8½ inches from the soffit of the lintel, and forms an architrave 2 feet 5 inches wide on the jambs. At the bottom of these are several figures, male and female, from 2 feet 1 inch to 2 feet 9 inches in height. On the lintel is Garuḍa grasping snakes in his hands—the *chinha* or cognizance of a Vaishṇava temple.

The roof in front of the door is carved with a fine Śesha or human-headed snake in the first compartment; and in the second is a circle of fishes with their heads turned towards the central knob (as in Cave II. at Badâmi), and round them is a ring of water plants.

From the side columns of the porch to the central beam, there have been brackets possibly like those in Cave III. at Badâmi, but they are now gone. The roof of the front of the porch or verandah has fallen and the two larger slabs (represented in photograph, Plate LIV.) now lying at the south-east corner of the temple probably formed part of this roof. The third seems to have been *recently* extracted from one of the niches in the wall, and was found lying near the gate, over some rods to keep them straight, and I had it set up where it appears in the photograph. The bold free style of these sculptures will strike the artist as quite unusual in Indian art. There are other similar slabs on the roof on each side of the porch, but portions of the stone have peeled off.

At the corner of the temple and partially sunk in the earth is a figure of a gigantic lion or monster with its paw on the back of a small elephant. This was also photographed.

The temple has once been enclosed in a court with gates: the south gate still remains and there are traces of the surrounding enclosure, but it has been divided by low walls built of the *débris*, and is used to store hay and straw and to shoot rubbish.

1. PLAN.

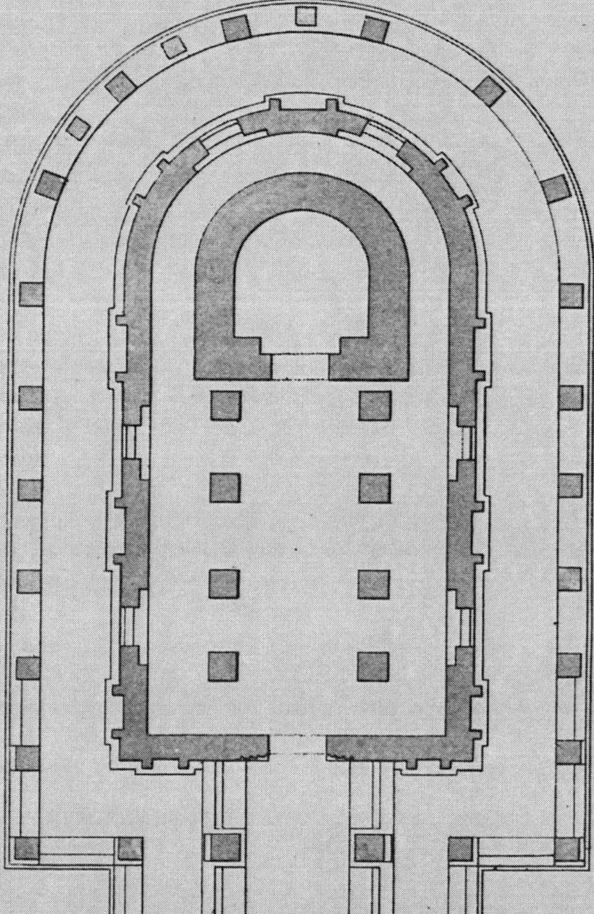

J. Burgess. delt.

Scale of Feet

3

2

4

D.M.

PLATE LIII.

AIWAḶḶI-PILLAR IN THE DURGA TEMPLE.

PLATE LIV.

AIWAḶḶI-SLABS OUTSIDE THE DURGA TEMPLE.

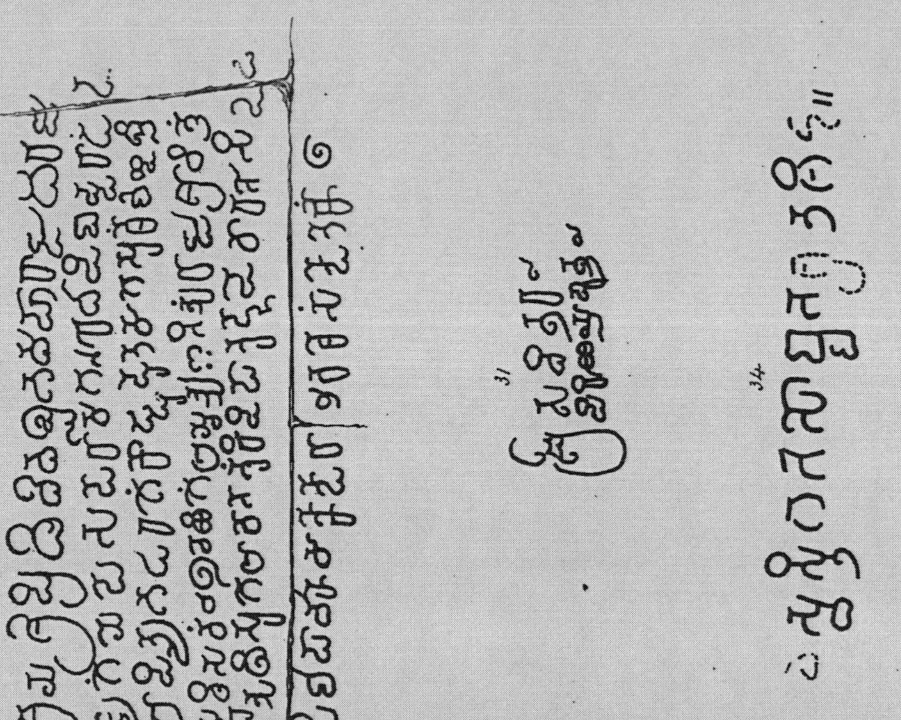

SNAKE STONES. PLATE LVI.

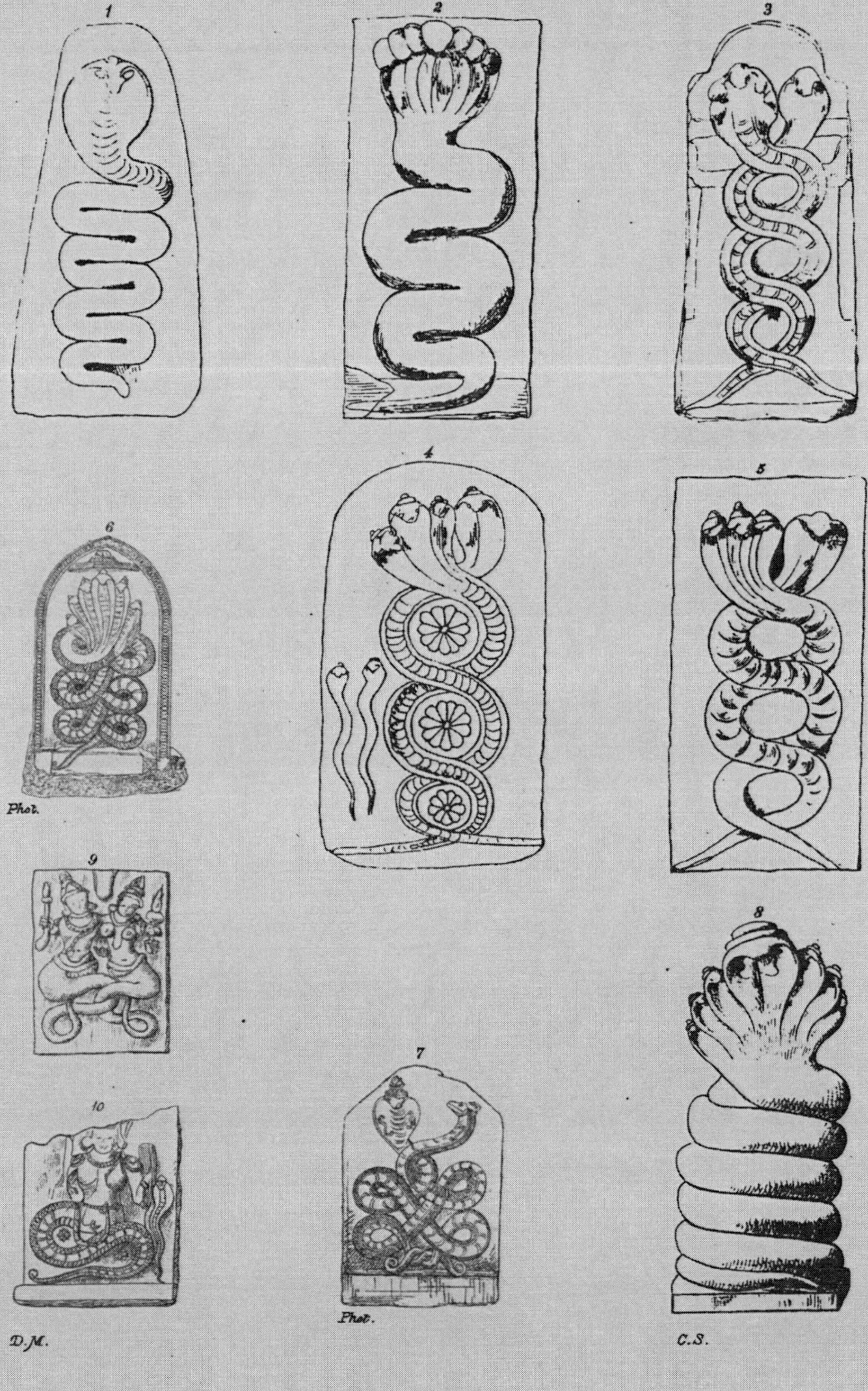

On the wall of the south gate are two inscriptions (Nos. 30 and 31, Plate LV.), the first beginning with the words:—*Svasti Vikramâditya Satyâśraya Srí Prithivívallabha mahârâjâdhirâja parameśvara bhatâra prithivírâjyageye.* The remainder is Kanarese, but as Vikramâditya died in 680 A.D. we have here a confirmation of the relation in which, from theoretical considerations, we should place this temple with regard to Cave III. at Badâmi.

This inscription was described by Col. Biggs as "on the gateway of the town," and photographed on a small scale—$3\frac{3}{10}$ inches being the length of the lines—so indistinctly that the late Dr. Bhâu Dâjî could make nothing of it. The second inscription, No. 31, is on the same wall lower down; and on a pillar in the temple is the inscription No. 32; while in the photograph Plate LIV. is a fourth one of a few letters on the base of the temple.

A considerable number of fine old temples in the village have been appropriated as dwellings, including the one with the inscription dated in 584 A.D. during the reign of Pulakeśi II.: one built of fine compact black stone seems to be used to clean cotton in. Of its beautiful columns, still almost unchipped, a photograph was taken.

To the south-west of the village, and at some distance from it, is a large collection of ruined temples which it would take a volume to illustrate fully. The weather, however, was oppressively hot and threatened rain, and there were 150 miles to be travelled across and three or four large rivers before reaching Solapur—so the work was closed on taking two more photographs—the first representing a fragment of an old gateway to the court of a temple; the second shewing a group of temples with a dolmen near one of them. Many other dolmens are scattered over the rocky ground to the south-west of these temples, and are probably more recent than the shrines.

Serpent Worship.

Wherever Śaiva worship prevails in Western India we find the serpent more or less venerated, and a collection of the sculptured representations of the forms employed would be interesting. At Konur, Huli, Sinde-Manauli, Badâmi, and Aiwaḷḷi there were many figures, some of them executed with considerable skill; and though some fine ones had to be passed over, a few specimens were sketched or photograped, and are represented in Plate LVI. Nos. 1 to 5 are from the court of the temple of Mâruti, in the village of Konur: No. 1 is a single snake on a slab 1 foot 10 inches high; 2 is a little larger, being 2 feet 3 inches high, and the snake having seven heads, the largest number usually assigned; No. 3 represents a pair on a slab 1 foot 8 inches high—the male with five heads, and the female, as usual, with only one; No. 4 is perhaps a more modern stone, 1 foot 5½ inches high, with a pair of snakes, the male in this case with three heads, and with them their two daughters; No. 5 is a similar pair: in both these last cases the serpents are crested. Nos. 6 and 7 are from a photograph of six sculptured stones in the principal temple at Sinde-Manauli, of which two were carved with nine figures each of Hindu *devas* or gods, seated in line; a third and fourth bore snakes similar to Nos. 1 and 5; the fifth, represented in No. 6, has a single serpent with seven heads (one of them broken off), very neatly carved,—each head has a crest, and over the whole is the *Chattra* or umbrella, emblematic of sovereignty; the sixth (No. 7) has a pair of crested snakes, the male only having its hood expanded. No. 8 is a sketch of a stone standing under a tree near the bank of the river outside Aiwaḷḷi, where the serpent is coiled round into the form of a short cylinder, with its seven-crested hoods expanding atop. Nos. 9 and 10 are from Huli, the first from the jamb of a temple door, the second from a slab. Some other examples were sketched, but have not been inserted in the plate for want of room.

PHOTOGRAPHS.

The following is a list of the Photographs taken :—

1.* Belgâm : Temple No. 1, outside the Commissariat Offices (I.).
2.* „ „ No. II., inside the Commissariat Compound (III.).
3.* „ „ „ roof of the manḍap (VI.).
4.* „ „ „ inner door (V.).
5. „ Gateway of the Fort.
6. Konur : Old temple at the village.
7.* „ Temple of Mahâlingeśvara from the north (IX.).
8. „ „ „ the west.
9. „ „ Inscription.
10. „ Falls of Gokâk and old temples above them.
11. „ Dolmen, No. 1, near the village.
12. „ „ No. 2, in the jungle.
13.* „ „ No. 3, in a field (XI.).
14. Kâdaroli : Old temple in the bed of the Mâlaprabhâ.
15. „ Inscribed stone or śilaśâśana, dated Śaka 997 (XIII.).
16. Sampgaṅw : Mosque.
17. Bail-Hangal : Old temple.
18. Saundati : Śilaśâśana.
19. Huli : Front of the temple of Panchalinga.
20.* „ Side view „ (XV.) (in duplicate).
21. „ Old temple on the hill.
22. „ Old temples near a tank.
23. Manauli : Temples of Panchalingeśvara.
24. „ Sculptured stones in the old temple.
25. „ A śilaśâśana.
26.* Badâmi : Cave I., the Front (XVII.).
27. „ „ eighteen armed Śiva.
28.* „ Cave II. (in duplicate) (XXI.).
29. „ „ Vishnu in the verandah.
30.* „ Cave III., from the north-east (XXIV.).
31. „ „ from the north-west (in duplicate).
32.* „ „ Pilaster and sculpture (XXVI.).
33. „ „ Garuḍa and figures over the entrance.
34.* „ „ west end of the verandah, Nṛiŝinha (XXIX.).
35.* „ „ east end of the verandah, Vishṇu (XXX.).

* Those marked with an asterisk * are published in this Report. The Roman numerals in parentheses indicate the number of the Plate.

36. Badâmi : Cave III. Varâha with Prithvi, &c.
37.* „ „ Vishnu as Virâṭrûpa, &c. (XXXI.)
38. „ Cave IV., the Jaina cave.
39. „ „ Parśvanâtha in the verandah.
40.* „ „ east end of the verandah (XXXVII.)
41. „ View of the old fort and temples (duplicate).
42.* Aiwaḷḷi : Brahmanical cave and monolith (L.)
43. „ „ figures in south corner.
44. „ „ „ north „
45. „ „ „ east „
46.* „ The Durga temple (LI.)
47.* „ „ Pillar in the porch (LIII.)
48. „ „ Door.
49.* „ „ Slabs outside (LIV.)
50. „ „ Siñha, &c.
51. „ „ Inscription.
52. „ Columns in a deserted temple.
53. „ Ruined gate to a temple.
54. „ Group of temples and dolmen.

The Plates in this Report contain reduced copies of most of the drawings made and Photo-lithographs of several of the impressions of inscriptions. Several other drawings could not be laid down to scale in time for publication, as I have to return to India immediately.

* Those marked with an asterisk * are published in this Report. The Roman numerals in parentheses indicate the number of the Plate.